P9-ELT-934

Fr Adolfo Nicolás and Fr Peter-Hans Kolvenbach

The Decrees and Documents of the Thirty-fifth General Congregation of the Society of Jesus

First published 2008
by Way Books, Campion Hall,
Oxford, OX1 1QS
www.theway.org.uk

Cover Design: Julian Littlewood

Colour photographs: Don Doll SJ,
with thanks to Peter Brook SJ

Printed in the United Kingdom by Hobbs the Printers Ltd

British Library Cataloguing-in-Publication Data

A catalogue record for this book is
available from the British Library

ISBN 978 0 904717 32 7

Contents

Abbreviations

AR	*Acta Romana Societatis Iesu*
Autobiography	*Reminiscences, or Autobiography of Ignatius Loyola*, translated by Philip Endean, in St Ignatius of Loyola, *Personal Writings* (Harmondsworth: Penguin, 1996)
Constitutions	*The Constitutions of the Society of Jesus and their Complementary Norms*, edited by John W. Padberg (St Louis: Institute of Jesuit Sources, 1996)
Exx	*The Spiritual Exercises of St Ignatius*, translated by George E. Ganss (St Louis: Institute of Jesuit Sources, 1992)
FGC	*Formula of a General Congregation* (Rome: General Curia, 1998)
GC 31 GC 32	*Documents of the 31st and 32nd General Congregations of the Society of Jesus*, edited by John W. Padberg (St Louis: Institute of Jesuit Sources, 1977)
GC 33	*Documents of the 33rd General Congregation of the Society of Jesus*, edited by Donald C. Campion and Albert C. Louapre (St Louis: Institute of Jesuit Sources, 1984)
GC 34	*Documents of the Thirty-fourth General Congregation of the Society of Jesus* (St Louis: Institute of Jesuit Sources, 1995)
GC 35	*Decrees and Documents of the Thirty-fifth General Congregation of the Society of Jesus* (Oxford: Way Books, 2008)
MHSI	*Monumenta Historica Societatis Iesu*
NC	*Normae Complementariae Constitutionum Societatis Iesu*, English text in *The Constitutions of the*

	Society of Jesus and their Complementary Norms, edited by John W. Padberg (St Louis: Institute of Jesuit Sources, 1996)
Vatican II	*Vatican Council II: The Conciliar and Post-conciliar Documents*, edited by Austin Flannery (New York: Costello, 1975)

All scripture quotations are taken from the New Revised Standard Version.

Curia Generalizia della Compagnia di Gesù
Borgo S. Spirito, 4
C.Fr 6139 00195 ROMA-PRATI (Italia)
Tel . 06/689.771—Fax 06/686.8214

General Congregation 35: Promulgation of the Decrees
2008/11
TO THE WHOLE SOCIETY

Dear Brothers in Christ,

Pax Christi!

In accordance with the Formula of a General Congregation n.142, and following the decision of General Congregation 35 taken during its concluding session on 6 March 2008, we have concluded all the tasks associated with the preparation of the decrees and documents of the General Congregation. This important and complex task was carried out with the wise counsel of the Assistants *ad providentiam* as well as of other members of the Curia with the right to take part in the affairs of a General Congregation.

The decrees of General Congregation 35 are effective as of today, the date of their promulgation.

On this occasion it is certainly fitting for us to pray in gratitude to the Lord who accompanied us during the time of the Congregation. These two months were marked by a sincere search for his will, deep communication with one another and fervent prayer. We were particularly blessed by our common morning prayer and our evening Eucharist. From our first session we implored the Lord for guidance and confirmation; we experienced his Spirit until the final Mass of Thanksgiving. At no time did we sense even a hint of resistance to what the Lord was asking of us. All of us in the Society are 'Friends in the Lord' and 'Servants of Christ's Mission', and the General Congregation has given us a clear witness of obedience to the Lord, to the Church and the Holy Father, and to our tradition and our way of proceeding.

The members of the General Congregation worked with unconditional dedication, a consequence, no doubt, of their awareness that in them the whole Society was truly present. The task now at hand lies with the whole Society. It is our responsibility to 'receive' the decrees and to give them life in our ministries, communities and personal lives. Our experience has taught us that the success or failure of a General Congregation does not lie in documents but in the quality of lives which are inspired by them. Because of this, I earnestly exhort all Jesuits to read, study, meditate on and appropriate these decrees. Likewise, I encourage you to enrich them with the depth of your own faith and insight. General Congregation 35 began a spiritual journey. As Ignatius would say, continue this journey in the Lord, always guided by his Spirit and in communion with our brother Jesuits throughout the world.

Certainly the recommendations and suggestions of the Congregation will shape the discernment and decisions of those of us at the General Curia. I am deeply aware of the expectations which the Congregation has raised and I am grateful to its members for providing me with an excellent and highly qualified team of counsellors and companions.

It is my earnest prayer that the Lord's abiding presence and the gift of his Spirit will help us to promote in the Society the way of proceeding which was experienced during General Congregation 35. I also pray that the process we have begun will produce abundant fruit in our ministries, in which we strive to bring the light of the gospel and living hope to all our brothers and sisters.

Sincerely in the Lord,

A. Nicolás SJ
Superior General

Rome, 30 May 2008
Solemnity of the Sacred Heart of Jesus

Historical Introduction

1. Preliminary Stages

The aim of this historical introduction is to help us to understand the important elements and the development of this 35th General Congregation from its convocation on 2 February 2006 until its conclusion on 6 March 2008.

On 2 February 2006, the feast of the Presentation of the Lord, Father General Peter-Hans Kolvenbach wrote to the whole Society that 'it had become more and more clear that the Society had arrived at a situation ... which required a General Congregation'.

Besides that, having obtained the agreement of His Holiness Benedict XVI and having heard the advice of the Assistants *ad providentiam* and of the Provincials of the whole Society, in accordance with the provision of Complementary Norm 362, §2 for the resignation of a Superior General, Fr Kolvenbach decided that the General Congregation must also be convened to provide for the supreme government of the Society. Consequently, he decreed the convocation of the 35th General Congregation for 5 January 2008 and added that it was the responsibility of Major Superiors to convoke and prepare Provincial Congregations which should conclude by 1 March 2007.

a. Remote Preparation

There is no doubt that the preparation of this 35th General Congregation had begun several years before its official convocation. Here are some milestones.

In September 2003, the 69th Procurators' Congregation met in Loyola. For several days the 85 Procurators had the opportunity to inform themselves about the lights and shadows of the universal body of the Society, thanks to the information given to them by the Father General, the Sectorial Secretaries, the General Councillors and the Secretary of the Society. Once in possession of this indispensable information, the Procurators were able to make a judgment on whether it was opportune or not to convoke a General Congregation.

The Congregation of Procurators has no legislative power at its disposal but it is perceived rather as a sort of enlarged consult of the Superior General. In 2003, it voted *non cogenda*, that is, that it was not in favour of imposing the convocation of a General Congregation. Nevertheless, it formulated a large number of proposals addressed to the central government of the Society and some recommendations in view of the next General Congregation.

In November 2005, a little over five years after the preceding meeting, Father General convoked a meeting of Major Superiors at Loyola. This was in conformity with what is stipulated by decree 23 of the 34th General Congregation, which asked the Superior General to convoke a meeting of all the Provincials about every six years, counting from the last General Congregation.

The purpose of the meeting in Loyola was to 'examine the state, the problems and the initiatives of the universal Society as well as international and supra-provincial collaboration'.[1]

The following themes were treated: the government of the Society, apostolic preferences, formation and collaboration with non-Jesuits. After a week of examination on the state of the Society, and after prayerful reflection and

[1] GC 34, decree 23, n. 486.

discussion on the different themes, the Provincials made numerous recommendations (21 in all) for the whole Society, independently of a General Congregation. Five recommendations, however, were retained as more important from the perspective of a General Congregation.

In a letter of 23 January 2006, Father General communicated to the whole Society these five recommendations from Loyola 2005:

> 1. The creation of a commission to study the new structures of government in the Society.
>
> 2. The creation of a commission to evaluate the implementation of the decree on collaboration with the laity.
>
> 3. An examination, by the General Congregation, of the quality of community life.
>
> 4. Attention by general government to the coherence and continuity of formation.
>
> 5. A study by the General Congregation of the question of Jesuit identity in relation to the mission in the Church and in today's world.

b. Immediate Preparation

In his official letter of convocation of the General Congregation, on 2 February 2006, Father General indicated that no particular subject for discussion had been laid down for the Provincial Congregations, but that it would be opportune if they should consider in their deliberations the five recommendations reserved by the Major Superiors at Loyola and also some questions raised in the allocution De statu societatis, especially at the end of that document.

The Provincial Congregations took place within the appointed time; they chose Electors and formulated postulates.

In the meantime, Father General, having examined with his consultors the recommendations voted at Loyola, decided upon and announced, in a letter of 7 July 2006, the creation of five preparatory commissions for the General Congregation. The task of these commissions was to study the themes likely to be treated by the General Congregation. The five commissions were as follows: social apostolate, juridical questions, collaboration with the laity, obedience, and community life. It was planned that these commissions would finish their work by the end of the year 2006 so that the fruits of their studies might be used by the *coetus praevius* of the 35th General Congregation, which would have its first meeting in March 2007.

All this preparation for the 35th General Congregation took place in the spiritual climate of the jubilee year, which began on 3 December 2005 in Xavier, at the end of the meeting of Major Superiors at Loyola. This jubilee, celebrating St Ignatius, St Francis Xavier and Blessed Pierre Favre, reminded the Society that, following the example of its founders and seeking evermore to live out the charism received from them, this same Society must have as its only desire to serve God our Lord, trusting that his Divine Majesty will be pleased to make use of it. It is worth remembering here that the General Congregation that had been convoked was of necessity a congregation *ad electionem.* As indicated earlier, the Holy Father had given his '*placet*' to Fr Kolvenbach and had allowed him to set in place the procedures which would lead to the presentation of his resignation. The latter took advantage of the meeting of Provincials in Loyola in 2005 to ask their opinion confidentially. They were unanimously in favour.

In order to help the future Electors of the General Congregation to prepare themselves to elect a new Superior General, Fr Kolvenbach, having taken advice from his councillors, wrote a letter on 29 June 2006 to all the Major Superiors, suggesting to them some common rules of conduct for the time leading up to the General Congregation and for the election of the new General. He asked the Moderators of the Assistancies to meet with the Major Superiors and the other future members of the 35th General Congregation who had the right to participate in the election. In a climate of spiritual discernment, the profile of the future General would be initially outlined. Then Fr Kolvenbach asked that the Electors suggest the names of some Jesuits who are professed of the Four Vows and who might be considered capable of assuming the office of Superior General. This was to be done in accordance with the profile and simply as some kind of indication, without entering into details.

One important clarification was communicated to the Electors in February 2007 concerning the mandate of the new General. A letter of Cardinal Bertone, Secretary of State, gave the answer of the Holy Father to the question which had been put to him: the mandate of the new General remains *ad vitam*; the norms concerning his right to summit his resignation remain in force.

On 20 February 2007, when all the Provincial Congregations had taken place, Father General convoked the *coetus praevius*, a commission charged with the immediate preparation of the General Congregation. The members of this commission were as follows: Father General *(ex officio)*, and Frs Lisbert D'Souza (General Councillor and coordinator of the *coetus*), Fratern Masawe (AOR), Eugène Goussikindey (AOC), Ernesto Cavassa (PER), Arturo Sosa (VEN), Peter Bisson (CSU), Thomas Smolich (CFN), Edward Mudavassery (HAZ), Stanislaus

Amalraj (AND), Adolfo Nicolás (JPN), Daniel Huang (PHI), Mark Rotsaert (BSE) and David Smolira (BRI). Fr Pasquale Borgomeo, at the request of Father General, was present at all the meetings of the *coetus praevius* as Secretary; he had previously read and classified all the postulates of the Provincial Congregations as well as those which came from particular groups or individuals.

c. The Work of the *coetus praevius*

This preparatory commission met in Rome from 15 March to 3 April 2007. Its principal task was to finish the immediate preparation of the Congregation by carefully analyzing all the postulates which had been received and by preparing some preliminary reports on the main questions which had been raised (FGC, 12, 2). The different reports were put together in a booklet entitled *Relationes praeviae*, which was given to the delegates before the General Congregation itself.

Three hundred and fifty postulates had been received by the General's curia and they were classified into three groups: those which must be passed on to the General Congregation, those which came within the competence of Father General (117) and those which were rejected (31). The first group formed the basis of the material prepared by the *coetus praevius*.

The postulates were classified into eleven themes and a *relatio praevia* was prepared for each theme. Within each *relatio* there was, first of all, a list of the postulates concerned with this particular theme. A summary stated what the postulates were asking for. Then the *coetus praevius* presented the state of the question, an analysis of the situation, an evaluation and finally some recommendations.

The *coetus praevius* also suggested dividing the groups of postulates into two categories: those which the

Congregation might deem likely to lead to a decree and those which could be discussed by the Congregation with a view to recommendations and mandates addressed to Father General and the ordinary government of the Society. The possible themes for an eventual decree were: mission, identity, government, obedience, and relations with the laity. The possible themes for ordinary government were: community life, formation, promotion of vocations, youth apostolate, and the Jesuit Refugee Service.

The *relationes praeviae,* translated into the three official languages (English, Spanish and French), were sent to all the Electors with a questionnaire so that they might think about them and answer the questions asked at the planned assistancy meetings. The *coetus praevius* met for a second time in Rome from 21 to 29 November 2007 in order to finish its work of examining the postulates that had been received since March, as well as the responses which had been sent to them from the Assistancies regarding the questions which had been put to them. The *coetus praevius* also proposed a schedule for the General Congregation.

After this second session, Father General sent to all the members of the General Congregation a letter, dated 12 December 2007, in which he informed them of the work of the *coetus praevius.* The commission was proposing a plan for five decrees:

> 1. An inspirational document to express our Jesuit identity and our charism.
>
> 2. A document on mission in order to reformulate the apostolic orientations of the 34th General Congregation (faith/justice, culture, dialogue).
>
> 3. Collaboration with others.
>
> 4. Apostolic obedience.
>
> 5. Leadership and governance.

The commission then proposed a list of twelve subjects concerning ordinary government. The commission also reflected upon the process and practical functioning of the Congregation so that the delegates' time might be put to the best possible use. It proposed a possible schedule, pointing out mainly that there would be two phases in the General Congregation: the first the election of the new General and the second the examination of some important questions affecting the universal Society and its mission. The first phase (*ad electionem*), devoted to the resignation of Father General, the study of the *De statu societatis* report and (once the resignation had been accepted) the election of the new Father General, would take about two weeks. During the second phase (*ad negotia*), Regional Assistants would be nominated, and the Assistants *ad providentiam* as well as the Admonitor of Father General would be elected. At the same time the *relationes praeviae* would be presented by the *coetus praeviae* and the Congregation would treat the questions proposed and would decide to vote on decrees or to give recommendations to Father General.

d. Other Aspects of the Preparation for the General Congregation

In the meantime, Father General had included the Provinces in the work of the preparation of the General Congregation by sending them some presentations on the different themes studied by the *coetus praevius.* These documents, as Fr Kolvenbach wrote in his letter of 4 September 2000 to the Major Superiors, aimed to allow communities to 'participate in the preparation [of the General Congregation] by prayer and reflection'.

Several other aspects of the preparation of the General Congregation which have not been touched on deserve to be mentioned here. Fr Josep Sugrañes, along with his collaborators, fulfilled an enormous task by taking care of reception, accommodation, logistics and a host of other details, before, during and after the Congregation. A range of facilities was put in place for the debates in the aula, for the translations, for the voting (a rapid and remarkably effective electronic system), for the distribution of texts (in three languages), and for communication with the Provinces. All of this presupposed the competent dedication of many people. Rules had been adopted concerning the communication of information to the outside and a team was set up to help with this. The daily prayers and special celebrations were also carefully prepared. In due course, the evaluation of the Congregation will tell of the high degree of satisfaction which was experienced with the preparations done, with the smooth functioning of arrangements and services and with the dedication of those looking after them.

2. *Opening of the 35th General Congregation*

a. The Opening Mass

The members of the 35th General Congregation arrived in Rome during the early days of January 2008. All were present on the morning of 7 January 2008 in the Church of the Gesù, the mother church of the Society, for the solemn opening Mass presided over by Cardinal Franc Rodé, Prefect of the Congregation for Institutes of Consecrated Life and Societies of Apostolic Life.

In his homily, the Cardinal, having recalled the aim of a General Congregation and the prospect of the election of a new General, addressed Fr Kolvenbach in these terms:

> I wish to express to you, Fr Kolvenbach, in my name and in the name of the Church, a heartfelt thanks for

> your fidelity, your wisdom, your righteousness and your example of humility and poverty.[2]

The rest of the homily was devoted to texts from the *Constitutions* and the *Spiritual Exercises* which treat of the Society's apostolic charism, of obedience to the Holy Father and of *sentire cum Ecclesia.*

The Cardinal concluded by issuing a strong invitation to the Jesuits:

> Despite the urgent apostolic needs, maintain and develop your charism to the point of being and showing yourselves to the world as 'contemplatives in action' who communicate to men and women and to all of creation the love received from God and to orientate them once again towards the love of God. Everyone understands the language of love.[3]

At the end of the celebration, Cardinal Rodé and Father General turned towards the altar of St Ignatius and, before the statue of the saint, Father General lit a lamp which, during the time of the General Congregation, symbolized the prayer of the whole Society throughout the world.

b. The Official Opening of the 35th General Congregation

At three o'clock in the afternoon of that same day, 7 January 2008, the members of the General Congregation met in assistancy groups to prepare for the official opening, which had been planned for four thirty. The task was to propose names for the election of members of the

[2] Franc Rodé, homily, 7 January 2008, § 3 (see below, 163–172).

[3] Rodé, homily, § 24.

commission *de statu* and for the positions of Secretary of the Election and his assistant.

The first session of the General Congregation was chaired by Fr Peter-Hans Kolvenbach. Two hundred and six Electors participated. In accordance with the Formula, the session began with the singing of the *Veni Creator.* Then Father General extended his welcome to the Electors and explained to them the reason for his presence as chairman. Pope Benedict XVI had asked Father General to remain in office until the moment when the General Congregation would accept his resignation and to continue as his delegate until the election of the new Superior General.

At the invitation of Father General, by a majority public vote, the General Congregation allowed ten Regional Superiors to take part in the General Congregation as Electors by right. These were the Superiors of the following regions: Amazonia, Cuba, Malaysia–Singapore, Mozambique, Nepal, East Timor, Puerto Rico, Russia, Rwanda–Burundi and Vietnam (the last region having been established as a Province after the convocation of the General Congregation).

Also, given the fact that the Provincial Congregation of Gujarat, which had the right to elect two Electors, had only elected one, it was decided by a public majority vote to admit Fr Fernando Fernández Franco as a second Elector. He was the substitute for the first Elector (FGC 35). These eleven fathers entered the aula, thus bringing the number of Electors to 217.

The Electors, in conformity with the Formula of the General Congregation, then decided by a public majority ballot that the Congregation could be considered as complete and legitimate. Father General then went on to the election of the Secretary of the Election and of his assistant. Fr Orlando Torres (Puerto Rico) was elected as Secretary and Fr Ignacio Echarte (Loyola) as his assistant.

Father General indicated the names of the Electors who formed the commission charged with judging cases of 'ambitioning' for the position of General. This commission is composed of the most senior members in religion from the ten Assistancies (FGC 54). Therefore they were Frs Augustin Karekezi (Africa), Ramón Alaix (South Latin America), Jorge Ambert (North Latin America), Jose Changanacherry (South Asia), Adolfo Nicolás (East Asia and Oceania), Wendelin Köster (Central Europe), Elías Royón (South Europe), Peter-Hans Kolvenbach (Western Europe), Adam Żak (Eastern Europe) and Vincent Cooke (United States of America).

Next came the elections of the constitution of the *deputatio de statu* responsible for gathering information and for submitting a report on the 'lights and shadows' in the Society. This commission included the four Assistants *ad providentiam* and ten members elected by the General Congregation, namely Frs Eugène Goussikindey (Africa), Alfonso Carlos Palacio (South Latin America), José Morales (North Latin America), Mudiappasamy Devadoss (South Asia), Bienvenido Nebres (East Asia and Oceania), Stefan Dartmann (Central Europe), Elías Royón (South Europe), Mark Rotsaert (Western Europe), Adam ˙Zak (Eastern Europe) and Bradley Schaeffer (United States of America).

Father General announced that the commission *de statu* would begin its work on the following day, 8 January 2008, under the chairmanship of Fr Valentín Menéndez, one of the Assistants *ad providentiam*.

The General Congregation was ready to begin its work. Father General then offered his resignation in these terms:

> With the blessing of the Holy Father granted the 20 June 2005, and after having obtained a positive vote from the Assistants for provident care and from the Provincials of the whole Society on the seriousness of the reasons to resign, I present now to the judgment of the General Congregation my resignation as Superior General of the Society of Jesus. As stated in article 362 of the Complementary Norms: although the Superior General is elected for life and not for any determined time, he may nonetheless in good conscience and by law resign from his office for a grave reason that would render him permanently unequal to the labours of his post. I feel that the Society of Jesus has the right to be governed and animated by a Jesuit in full capacity of his spiritual and corporal gifts and not by a companion whose energies will continue to diminish because of his age—soon eighty years old—and because of the consequences of that age, especially in the area of health. Even if the *Constitutions* and the *Norms* do not mention it, may I add that the election of a new General will give the Society God's grace of renewal, or to express it with the words of Saint Ignatius '*una nueva devoción*', '*nuevas mociones*'. The discussion and the vote on the resignation will take place at the eve of the four days of *murmurationes* which will be determined by the deputation *de statu Societatis*. In a less formal and a more fraternal way the decision of the General Congregation will be communicated to the whole Society. So much for the resignation.

Father General read the letter of the Holy Father by which the Sovereign Pontiff gave his blessing to the General Congregation. The Congregation then accepted the proposal of Father General to assign to Fr Jacques Gellard the task of giving an exhortation on the same day as the election. In conclusion Father General recited the prayer to the Holy Spirit.

The debate and the vote of the Congregation on the resignation were fixed for Monday 14 January 2008.

Everything happened in the presence of a statue of St Ignatius given by the Province of English Canada and placed beside the President's table. Thus the 35th General Congregation was launched, committed to discern, by the light of the Spirit, what must today 'be determined for the greater glory of God'.

3. *Beginning the Work of the Congregation*

From 8 to 12 January 2008, the commission *de statu* carried on its work while the other members of the Congregation held meetings in language or assistancy groups to discuss the *relationes praeviae* of the *coetus praevius,* in preparation for the second phase *(ad negotia)* of the General Congregation.

On 14 January, in plenary session, the Congregation submitted the resignation of Father General to the vote. First the signed letter sent to Fr Kolvenbach by the Holy Father was read. Then Fr Menéndez, the Moderator, invited the Electors who wished to do so to put questions to the four Assistants *ad providentiam* on the reasons for the resignation of Father General. This time for questions was followed by a moment of silent individual prayer before proceeding to the ballot.

Father General, who had left the aula during the ballot, was invited to return to learn the result of the ballot. The Congregation had accepted the reasons which had led him to present his resignation. Fr Menéndez, in moving terms and in the name of the whole Society, thanked him for his 25 years as General at the service of the Society. In his turn Fr Kolvenbach thanked the delegates and concluded:

> On this eve of the election of my successor and of the many decisions that the General Congregation will

have to make, I unite myself with the prayer with which St Ignatius finished his letters: 'May God our Lord in his infinite and supreme goodness be pleased to give us his abundant grace, so that we may know his most holy will and entirely fulfil it'.[4]

4. *The Election of the Superior General*

After four days of prayer, reflection and consultation among themselves (*murmurationes*), the 217 Electors of the 35th General Congregation were ready, on the morning of 19 January 2008, to proceed to the election of the new General.

Under the chairmanship of Fr Frank E. Case, Secretary of the Society, they concelebrated the Mass of the Holy Spirit in the nearby Church of the Holy Spirit in Sassia. When this was over, the Electors went immediately into the aula of the Congregation, where there were enclosed. After the prayer *Veni Creator*, they listened to the exhortation of Fr Jacques Gellard (Assistant *ad providentiam*). Then in silence each of the Electors continued in prayer until the end of the first hour of the session. Each Elector then wrote, in his own hand, on a printed ballot sheet, the name of the one whom he chose as General.

By a majority of votes, Fr Adolfo Nicolás was elected, from the Province of Japan. Former Provincial of Japan, he had been for three years President of the Conference of Major Superiors of East Asia and Oceania.

The decree of appointment was immediately drawn up by the Secretary of the Congregation and signed by Fr Peter-Hans Kolvenbach as delegate of the Holy Father.

[4] Peter-Hans Kolvenbach, letter to the Society, 14 January 2008, § 6 (see below, 161–162).

The newly elected General approached the crucifix in the centre of the aula and pronounced the profession of faith.

The name of the elected was immediately communicated to the Holy Father.

Then, after Fr Kolvenbach, the Secretary and his assistant, all the Electors approached the newly elected General to greet him. After this demonstration of respect and affection, the doors of the aula were opened and the members of the community of the curia came to greet the General.

A Mass of Thanksgiving was celebrated the day after the election, Sunday 20 January, in the Church of the Gesù, in the presence of a great number of Jesuits as well as members of numerous religious congregations.

Some days later, on Saturday 26 January, in the morning, Pope Benedict XVI received the newly elected General in private audience. It was a brief and cordial meeting in the course of which, according to the custom of the Society, Father General renewed his vow of obedience to the Holy Father.

5. *The Phase* **ad negotia** *of the 35th General Congregation*

a. Organization

As laid down in the Formula, once the election of the General had been completed, the Congregation started the second phase *ad negotia*. The Congregation began by electing a Secretary and two Assistants. Fr Mark Rotsaert (North Belgium) was elected as Secretary of the Congregation, and Frs Ignacio Echarte (Loyola) and Thomas Smolich (California) as his Assistants.

Next came the elections to form the *deputatio ad negotia,* a commission responsible for helping Father General to organize the work of the Congregation. Ten members coming from ten Assistancies were elected:

Jean-Roger Ndombi (West Africa), Ernesto Cavassa (Peru), George Pattery (Calcutta), Arturo Sosa (Venezuela), Daniel Huang (Philippines), János Lukács (Hungary), Lluis Magriñà (Tarragona), František Hylmar (Bohemia), François-Xavier Dumortier (France) and Thomas Smolich (California).

Three members of this *deputatio* were chosen to be Moderators of the general sessions: Frs Ndombi, Huang and Magriñà. A smaller coordinating committee was also set up: Frs Cavassa, Dumortier, Pattery and Smolich.

On 23 January the General Congregation clarified the manner of proceeding in order to treat the different themes in language groups. Twenty-one groups were formed in this way to treat the five themes of possible decrees proposed by the *coetus praevius*: ten groups for mission and identity, three for the theme of the government of the Society, three for apostolic obedience and five for collaboration with others. On 24 January the different groups sent a written report back to the Secretary indicating the principal points raised in the discussion. Included in the report were a preliminary draft of a document on the subject discussed and an indication of the 'tone' which the decree should adopt.

b. The New Team around Father General

After the election of Fr Nicolás, the General Congregation devoted some days to the question of the constitution of a new team around Father General. First, the manner of proceeding had to be clarified. The 34th General Congregation, in its decree 23 (section E II) had adopted, on an experimental basis, a procedure for the appointment of General Councillors and for the election of Assistants *ad providentiam*. It had also envisaged a revision of this procedure by the following General Congregation.

Information was then given on the actual sharing of responsibilities and on the tasks of Councillors, Regional Assistants and Assistants *ad providentiam.* The Electors exchanged ideas on this, and by a vote which took place on 28 January, decided to maintain the system of government and the election procedure of the members of Father General's Council adopted by the 34th General Congregation.

The Electors of each Assistancy proposed to Father General the names of three candidates who were members of their Assistancy and who would be suitable to become General Councillors and to be appointed Regional Assistants.

Consequently on 12 February the following General Councillors and Regional Assistants were appointed by Father General:

Fr Jean-Roger Ndombi (West Africa): Assistant for Africa

Fr Marcos Recolons (Bolivia): Assistant for Southern Latin America

Fr Gabriel Ignacio Rodríguez (Colombia): Assistant for Northern Latin America

Fr Lisbert D'Souza (Bombay): Assistant for South Asia

Fr Daniel Huang (Philippines): Assistant for East Asia and Oceania

Fr Adam Żak (Southern Poland): Assistant for Central and Eastern Europe

Fr Joaquín Barrero Díaz (Castille): Assistant for Southern Europe

Fr Antoine Kerhuel (France): Assistant for Western Europe

Fr James E. Grummer (Wisconsin): Assistant for the United States of America

Since a single Assistant is now responsible for Central Europe and Eastern Europe, the number of Regional Assistants went from ten to nine.

On 14 February Father General introduced something new: the appointment of two General Councillors non-resident in Rome, Fr Mark Rotsaert (President of the Conference of European Provincials) and Fr Arturo Sosa (Rector of the Catholic University of Táchira, Venezuela).

Finally, on 18 February, the General Congregation elected the four Assistants *ad providentiam* (FGC, 130–137): Frs Lisbert D'Souza, James E. Grummer, Federico Lombardi and Marcos Recolons. It then elected Fr Marcos Recolons as Admonitor to Father General (FGC, 138–141).

Fr General appointed two other General Councillors: Fr Orlando Torres (Puerto Rico), confirmed as General Councillor for Formation, and Fr Joseph Daoust, Delegate for the Inter-provincial Houses of Rome. Then Father General appointed Fr Ignacio Echarte (Loyola) Secretary of the Society, replacing Fr Frank E. Case.

6. *The Documents*

a. The Method of Treating the Work

Independently of the appointments mentioned above, the General Congregation continued its work, still using the same method for dealing with subjects with a view to voting decrees. Commissions were set up to work on various themes and to present them in the aula. Each Assistancy then met to react, to prepare remarks and to present them in plenary assembly. The commissions gathered and evaluated the suggestions and commentaries in order to draft a second report and a text for a decree. This was presented in the assembly and followed by questions for clarification and discussion. Eventually there came a final draft to which amendments in writing could be proposed. The assembly then moved to a final vote on these amendments and on the text of the decree in its totality.

In certain cases, after discussion in the aula, the draft text had to be re-examined by an editing committee. A new presentation and a new discussion followed. In this way the Congregation as a whole worked together to improve texts by observations and suggestions presented in the aula or sent in writing to the various commissions responsible for the drafting of the decrees.

b. The Decrees

Five commissions worked on drafting the documents which were voted on and accepted as decrees on the following subjects:

1. Identity: a fire that kindles other fires: rediscovering our charism.
2. Challenges for our mission today: sent to the frontiers.
3. Obedience in the life of the Society.
4. Governance at the service of universal mission.
5. Collaboration at the heart of the mission.

It should be further noted, however, that a sixth commission was set up to write and propose a response from the Society to the letter of Pope Benedict XVI to Fr Kolvenbach (10 January 2008)—to which the latter had replied on 15 January—as well as to the Pope's speech to the members of the Congregation during the audience on

21 February.[5] This *ad hoc* commission worked in various stages and produced the document 'With Renewed Vigour and Zeal', in which the General Congregation and the Society expressed their gratitude to the Holy Father for his esteem and trust as well as their response to his call.

c. Subjects Entrusted to the Ordinary Government of the Society

From the beginning the 35th General Congregation, in harmony with the proposals of the *coetus praevius*, had expressed its desire not to produce a large number of documents. Nevertheless it touched on many other subjects which were not destined to be developed into decrees but which were presented by a commission, freely discussed by the delegates and sent to Father General, usually in the form of suggestions or recommendations, for the ordinary government of the Society.

The following are the subjects which were dealt with in this manner and which are presented together in another document: youth ministry, migrants, dialogue and religious fundamentalism, the intellectual apostolate, communications, ecology, formation, community life, finances, Africa, China, the Roman Houses, Jesuit Brothers and indigenous peoples.[6]

7. The Papal Audience

On 21 February 2008, in response to an invitation from the Holy Father, all the members of the General Congregation made their way to the Vatican and went to the *Sala Clementina*, where they were received in audience at 12.15 by His Holiness Pope Benedict XVI. Father

5 See below, 135–140, 141–147, 148–151.

6 See below, 121–131.

General addressed to him some words of greeting and gratitude. The Holy Father, in his speech to the General Congregation, reaffirmed his trust in the Society and encouraged it in its present mission in terms which deeply moved the members of the Congregation:

> I therefore ardently hope that thanks to the results of your Congregation the entire Society of Jesus will be able to live out with renewed dynamism and fervour the mission for which the Spirit willed it in the Church and has preserved it for more than four and a half centuries with extraordinary apostolic fruitfulness. Today, in the ecclesial and social context that marks the beginning of this millennium, I would like to encourage you and your confrères to continue on the path of this mission in full fidelity to your original charism ... the Church needs you, relies on you and continues to turn to you with trust ....[7]

8. *Conclusion: The End of the General Congregation*

On 1 March in the aula, in a special ceremony which was simple and short but very warm, Father General expressed in the name of the entire Society the gratitude owed to Fr Peter-Hans Kolvenbach for his almost 25 years of service to the universal Society as Superior General. The whole assembly stood up and applauded at length, thus expressing their profound appreciation. The General Congregation also approved the text of a letter of thanks to Fr Kolvenbach.

On Wednesday 5 March, at the end of the afternoon plenary session, Father General thanked the assembly and formulated some recommendations. On Thursday 6 March, four members of the General Congregation gave

[7] Benedict XVI, allocution to the 35th General Congregation of the Society of Jesus, 21 February 2008, § 2 (see below, 141–147).

witness to their experience of these two months of General Congregation.

Then the delegates voted unanimously to renounce the right to have three days for intercessions (FGC 125). After a pause, the assembly by a large majority voted the powers granted to Father General for the promulgation of the authorised text of the decrees, as soon as the necessary corrections have been made. Thus the 35th General Congregation officially ended.

Father General thanked the Brothers for their participation in the work of the General Congregation. He also thanked the translators, the two Secretaries of the Congregation, the assistant secretaries, the Moderators, the members of the *deputatio*, the *ad hoc* commission, the liturgical team, the media technicians, the treasurer's office, the infirmary and the entire Curia staff.

On the afternoon of the same day, the delegates and all those who had helped them met once again in the Church of the Gesù to celebrate the final Eucharist, which had been carefully prepared by the liturgical team. The *Te Deum* was sung at the end of the Mass (FGC, 143).

In his homily, Father General said in conclusion:

> I believe that we are all aware that we have had a great experience. The Word of God, however, invites us to go to the source of this experience and to make sure that it is being transformed into mission, an all-embracing mission, a mission which will continue to bear fruit in others.[8]

(original in French)

[8] Adolfo Nicolás, homily, final Mass, 6 March 2008, § 13 (see below, 179–185).

Decrees of the General Congregation

DECREE 1: 'With Renewed Vigour and Zeal'

The Society of Jesus responds to the invitation of the Holy Father

I. A Spiritual Experience of Consolation in the Lord

1. The 35th General Congregation experienced the deep affection of the Holy Father on two occasions, in his letter of 10 January 2008 and at the audience on 21 February 2008. Following in the footsteps of St Ignatius and his companions, we gathered, the 225 delegates led by our Father General, Adolfo Nicolás, as the General Congregation of the Society of Jesus, to be hosted by the Vicar of Christ and to listen with open hearts to what he would say about our mission. It was a powerful moment and a moving spiritual experience. In his address, Pope Benedict XVI openly revealed his confidence in the Society of Jesus, as well as his spiritual closeness and deep esteem, in words that touched our hearts, stirring and inspiring our desire to serve the Church in this contemporary world marked 'by many complex social, cultural and religious challenges'.[1]

2. These two events gave new clarity to the challenging task of the General Congregation. After the election of our Superior General, the largest part of our work was actually devoted to issues concerning our identity, our religious life and our mission. As is its duty, the General Congregation attentively scrutinised the situation of our apostolic body in order to provide guidance that will enhance and increase the spiritual and

[1] Benedict XVI, letter to Fr Peter-Hans Kolvenbach, 10 January 2008, §3 (see below, 135–140).

evangelical quality of our way of being and proceeding. First in importance is our intimate union with Christ, 'the secret of the authentic success of every Christian's apostolic and missionary commitment, and especially of those who are called to a more direct service of the gospel'.[2]

3. Our effort to be completely honest with ourselves and with the Lord included much of the dynamic of the First Week of the Spiritual Exercises: it helped us discover and recognise our weaknesses and inconsistencies but also the depth of our desire to serve. This required that we re-examine our attitudes and our way of living.

4. However, this experience could not lose sight of the perspective that grounds it: our mission. Indeed, the transition from the First to the Second Week of the Exercises is a change in perspective: the retreatant experiences how his entire life has been embraced with mercy and forgiveness, ceases to concentrate on himself, and starts to 'gaze upon Christ our Lord, the eternal King, and all the world assembled before him. He calls to them all and to each person in particular.'[3] Truly we are sinners and 'yet called to be companions of Jesus as Ignatius was'.[4]

5. For the delegates this was the spiritual effect of the allocution of the Holy Father at the audience on 21 February. In presenting to us with deep affection a dynamic vision of our mission and our service to the Church, he seemed to say: 'turn your gaze to the future "to respond to the expectations that the Church has of you"'.[5]

[2] Benedict XVI, letter, §2.

[3] Exx, 95.

[4] GC 32, decree 2, n.1.

[5] Benedict XVI, allocution, §1.

II. Confirmed and Sent on Mission

6. With such powerful words, the Holy Father definitively placed the future of our mission before us, a mission expressed with complete clarity and firmness: the defence and proclamation of the faith, which leads us to discover new horizons and to reach new social, cultural and religious frontiers. As Fr Adolfo Nicolás noted in his words to the Holy Father, these frontiers can be places of conflict and tension that threaten our reputation, our peace and our security. That is why we were so moved by the Pope's evocation of the memory of Fr Arrupe. The Holy Father referred to his proposal that Jesuits be in service to refugees as 'one of [his] last far-sighted intuitions'.[6] The service of faith and the promotion of justice must be kept united. Pope Benedict reminded us that the injustice that breeds poverty has 'structural causes',[7] which must be opposed, and that the source of this commitment can be found in the faith itself: 'the preferential option for the poor is implicit in the Christological faith in the God who has become poor for us, so as to enrich us with his poverty (cf. 2 Corinthians 8:9)'.[8] By sending us to 'the physical and spiritual places where others do not reach or have difficulty in reaching',[9] the Pope entrusts to us the task to 'build bridges of understanding and dialogue',[10] according to the best tradition of the Society, in the diversity of its ministries:

> In its history, the Society of Jesus has lived extraordinary experiences of proclamation and encounter between the Gospel and world cultures—it suffices to

6 Benedict XVI, allocution, § 8.

7 Benedict XVI, allocution, § 8.

8 Benedict XVI, allocution, § 8.

9 Benedict XVI, allocution, § 2.

10 Benedict XVI, allocution, § 5.

> think of Matteo Ricci in China, Roberto De Nobili in India or of the 'Reductions' in Latin America. And you are rightly proud of them. I feel it is my duty today to urge you to set out once again in the tracks of your predecessors with the same courage and intelligence, but also with an equally profound motivation of faith and enthusiasm to serve the Lord and his Church.[11]

In a decisive manner Benedict XVI confirmed what our previous General Congregations have said of our specific mission of service to the Church.

7. In this light we can better understand why the Pope stresses so much—in his letter and in his allocution—that 'the Church's evangelizing work therefore relies heavily on the Society's responsibility for formation in the fields of theology, spirituality and mission'.[12] In an era of complex social, cultural and religious challenges, the Pope asks us faithfully to help the Church. This fidelity demands serious and rigorous research in the theological field and in dialogue with the contemporary world, cultures and religions. What the Church expects from us is sincere collaboration in the search for the full truth to which the Spirit leads us, in full adherence to the faith and the teaching of the Church. This help and this service are not confined to our theologians; they extend to all Jesuits, called to act with great pastoral sensitivity in the variety of our missions and apostolic work. They are manifest also in the institutions of the Society as a characteristic of their identity.

[11] Benedict XVI, allocution, § 5.

[12] Benedict XVI, letter, § 6.

III. The Response of the Society to the Call of the Holy Father

8. It is obvious that the Society cannot let this historic moment pass without giving a response at the same high level as the ecclesial charism of St Ignatius. The Successor of Peter told us of the confidence he has in us; for our part, we sincerely want to respond to him, as an apostolic body, with the same warmth and the same affection he has shown us, and to affirm in a resolute way our specific availability to the 'Vicar of Christ on earth'.[13] The 35th General Congregation expresses its full adherence to the faith and the teaching of the Church, as they are presented to us in the intimate relationship that unites Scripture, Tradition and the Magisterium.[14]

9. The 35th General Congregation calls all Jesuits to live with the great spirit and generosity that is at the centre of our vocation:

> ... to serve as a soldier of God beneath the banner of the Cross ... and to serve the Lord alone and the Church his spouse, under the Roman Pontiff, the Vicar of Christ on earth.[15]

10. From the beginning of our formation and throughout our lives we must be and remain men familiar with the things of God. Our desire is to grow now and in the future in the 'interior knowledge of Our Lord, who became human for me, that I may love him more intensely and follow him more closely',[16] especially in prayer and in

[13] Formula of the Institute, *Constitutions*, 1.

[14] Cf. Vatican II, *Dei verbum*, 7–10 and the instruction *Donum veritatis*, 6, 13–14.

[15] Formula of the Institute, *Constitutions*, 1.

[16] Exx, 104.

community life and in apostolic work. As Nadal said, '*La Compañía es fervor*'.[17]

11. As we know, 'mediocrity has no place in Ignatius' world view'.[18] It is therefore essential to give young Jesuits a human, spiritual, intellectual and ecclesial formation as deep, strong and vibrant as possible to allow each of them to achieve our mission in the world with 'a proper attitude of service in the Church'.[19]

12. To be authentically 'contemplatives in action', seeking and finding God in all things, we must continually return to the spiritual experience of the Spiritual Exercises. Aware that they are 'a gift which the Spirit of the Lord has made to the entire Church', we should, as we are called by the Holy Father, 'reserve a specific attention to the ministry of the Spiritual Exercises'.[20]

13. We are aware of the importance of the intellectual apostolate for the life and mission of the Church today, as Pope Benedict XVI has told us on several occasions since the beginning of his pontificate. We have heard his appeal and want to respond fully. In this context, we encourage our theologians to carry out their task with courage and intelligence; as we have heard the Holy Father say:

> This is not, of course, a simple task, especially when one is called to proclaim the gospel in very different social and cultural contexts and is obliged to address different mindsets.[21]

[17] Jerónimo Nadal, *Plática 3ª en Alcalá* (1561), § 60 (MHSI 90, 296).

[18] Peter-Hans Kolvenbach, 'To Friends and Colleagues of the Society of Jesus', *AR*, 20 (1991), 606.

[19] GC 34, decree 11.

[20] Benedict XVI, allocution, § 9.

[21] Benedict XVI, letter, § 5.

Given the difficulties inherent in the task of evangelization in our time, it is important that they are disposed,

> ... in the most genuine Ignatian spirit of 'feeling with the Church and in the Church'—'to love and serve' the Vicar of Christ on earth with that 'effective and affective devotion' which must make you his invaluable and irreplaceable collaborators in his service for the universal Church.[22]

To be missioned to this work at the new frontiers of our times always requires that we also be rooted at the very heart of the Church. This tension, specific to the Ignatian charism, opens the way to true creative fidelity.

14. In the light of decree 11 of the 34th General Congregation and the final speech of Fr Peter-Hans Kolvenbach to the Congregation of Procurators in September 2003, we call each Jesuit to consider 'the proper attitude of service in the Church', which should be ours. This means recognising, with honesty to ourselves and before God, that some of our reactions and our attitudes have not always been expressed as our Institute demands of us: to be 'men humble and prudent in Christ'.[23] We regret this, conscious of our common responsibility as an apostolic body. Therefore, we call on each Jesuit, with a resolutely constructive attitude, to strive, with the Holy Father, to create a spirit of 'communion' so that the Church can bring the gospel of Christ to a world as complex and troubled as ours.

15. Recalling the Examen[24] and asking the Lord for the grace of conversion, we ask each of our companions to examine his own way of living and working at 'the new

[22] Benedict XVI, allocution, § 7.

[23] Formula of the Institute, *Constitutions*, 9.

[24] Exx, 32–43.

frontiers of our time'. This examination will include the following: the demands of our mission 'among the poor and with the poor'; our commitment to the ministry of the Spiritual Exercises; our concern for the human and Christian formation of a complete cross section of individuals; 'that harmony with the Magisterium which avoids causing confusion and dismay among the People of God'[25] about the 'themes, continuously discussed and called into question today, of the salvation of all humanity in Christ, of sexual morality, of marriage and the family'.[26] Each Jesuit is invited to acknowledge humbly his mistakes and faults, to ask the Lord's grace to help him live his mission and, if necessary, the grace of forgiveness.

16. The letter and the allocution of the Holy Father open for us a new epoch. The General Congregation gives us the opportunity to live 'with renewed dynamism and fervour the mission for which the Spirit willed it [the Society] in the Church'.[27] Conscious of our responsibility, in, with, and for the Church, we desire to love it more and help others love it more, for it leads the world to Christ humble and poor and announces to every person that *Deus caritas est*.[28] We cannot separate the love of Christ from this 'sense of the Church',[29] which leads 'the entire Society to seek to integrate itself more and more vigorously and creatively in the life of the Church so that we may experience and live its mystery within ourselves'.[30]

17. We acknowledge what the Lord calls us to be and to live with greater intensity, through the letter of the Holy Father on 10 January and his address at the audience on 21

[25] Benedict XVI, allocution, § 6.

[26] Benedict XVI, allocution, § 6.

[27] Benedict XVI, allocution, § 2.

[28] Benedict XVI, encyclical, *Deus caritas est*.

[29] Exx, 352–370.

[30] GC 33, decree 1, n. 8.

February. 'In the spirit of the Fourth Vow *in regard to missions* that so distinctively unites us with the Holy Father',[31] we want to express our willingness to achieve what he invites us to put into practice and what he encourages us to continue or to initiate. We express our renewed availability to be sent into the Lord's vineyard for the greater service of the Church and the greater glory of God. In asking the Lord for the power of his Spirit to do his will, all of us unite our voices to that of the Successor of Peter in praying with him:

> Take, Lord, and receive all my liberty, my memory, my understanding and all my will—all that I have and possess. You, Lord, have given all that to me. I now give it back to you, O Lord. All of it is yours. Dispose of it according to your will. Give me love of yourself along with your grace, for that is enough for me.[32]

(original in Spanish)

[31] GC 34, decree 11, n. 18.

[32] Exx, 234.

DECREE 2: A Fire that Kindles Other Fires: Rediscovering our Charism

Many Sparks, One Fire: Many Stories, One History

1. The Society of Jesus has carried a flame for nearly 500 years through innumerable social and cultural circumstances that have challenged it intensely to keep that flame alive and burning. Things are no different today. In a world that overwhelms people with a multiplicity of sensations, ideas and images, the Society seeks to keep the fire of its original inspiration alive in a way that offers warmth and light to our contemporaries. It does this by telling a story that has stood the test of time, despite the imperfections of its members and even of the whole body, because of the continued goodness of God, who has never allowed the fire to die. Our attempt here is to present it anew as a living narrative that, when brought into contact with the life stories of people today, can give them meaning and provide focus in a fragmented world.

2. The continued narrative of the Society has provided, over the centuries, the ground for numerous experiences of unity-in-multiplicity. We Jesuits are frequently surprised that, despite our differences in culture and context, we find ourselves remarkably united. Through prayerful discernment, open discussion and spiritual conversations we have again and again been privileged to know ourselves as one in the Lord:[1] one united, apostolic body seeking what is best for the service of God in the Church and for the world. This graced experience reminds us of the experience recounted in the Deliberation of the First Fathers. Our earliest companions, even though they considered themselves weak and fragile and originating from many different places, found the will of God

[1] Cf. *Constitutions*, VIII. 1. 8 [671].

together amid great diversity of opinion.[2] What enabled them to find God's will was their 'decided care and alertness to initiate a completely open way' and to offer themselves fully to it for the greater glory of God.[3] Thus they began a narrative: they lit a fire, which was handed on in subsequent generations whenever people encountered the Society, enabling the personal histories of generations to become embedded in the Society's history as a whole. This collective history formed the basis of their unity; and at its heart was Jesus Christ. Despite the differences, what unites us as Jesuits is Christ and the desire to serve him: not to be deaf to the call of the Lord, but prompt and ready to do his most holy will.[4] He is the unique image of the unseen God,[5] capable of revealing himself everywhere; and in a tantalising culture of images, he is the single image that unites us. Jesuits know who they are by looking at him.

3. We Jesuits, then, find our identity not alone but in companionship: in companionship with the Lord, who calls, and in companionship with others who share this call. Its root is to be found in St Ignatius' experience at La Storta. There, 'placed' with God's Son and called to serve him as he carries his Cross, Ignatius and the First Companions respond by offering themselves for the service of faith to the Pope, Christ's Vicar on earth. The Son, the one image of God, Christ Jesus, unites them and sends them out to the whole world. He is the image at the very heart of Jesuit existence today; and it is his image that we wish to communicate to others as best we can.

[2] Deliberation of the First Fathers (1539), §1 (MHSI 63, 2).

[3] Deliberation, §1 (MHSI 63, 2).

[4] Exx, 91.

[5] 2 Corinthians 4:4; Colossians 1:15; Hebrews 1:3.

Seeing and Loving the World as Jesus Did

4. Fundamental for the life and mission of every Jesuit is an experience that places him, quite simply, with Christ at the heart of the world.[6] This experience is not merely a foundation laid in the past and ignored as time moves on; it is alive, ongoing, nourished and deepened by dynamic Jesuit life in community and on mission. The experience involves both conversion from and conversion for. St Ignatius, recuperating on his bed at Loyola, entered into a profound interior journey. He gradually came to realise that those things in which he took delight had no lasting value, but that responding to Christ's beckoning instilled peace in his soul and a desire to know his Lord better. But—as he came to see later—this knowledge could only be won through confronting the falseness of the desires that had driven him. It was at Manresa that this confrontation took place. There the Lord, who taught him like a schoolboy, gently prepared him to receive an understanding that the world could be seen in another way: a way freed from disordered attachments[7] and opened up for an ordered loving of God and of all things in God. This experience is part of every Jesuit's journey.

5. While at Manresa, Ignatius had an experience at the river Cardoner that opened his eyes so that 'all things seemed new to him'[8] because he began to see them with new eyes.[9] Reality became transparent to him, enabling him to see God working in the depths of everything and inviting him to 'help souls'. This new view of reality led Ignatius to seek and find God in all things.

6 Cf. *NC*, 246, 4°; 223 §§ 3–4.

7 Exx, 21.

8 *Autobiography*, 30.

9 Diego Laínez, letter about Fr Ignatius (1547), § 10 (MHSI 66, 80).

6. The understanding that Ignatius received taught him a contemplative way of standing in the world, of contemplating God at work in the depths of things, of tasting 'the infinite sweetness and charm of the divinity, of the soul, of its virtues and of everything there'.[10] Starting from the contemplation of the incarnation[11] it is clear that Ignatius does not sweeten or falsify painful realities. Rather he begins with them, exactly as they are—poverty, forced displacement, violence between people, abandonment, structural injustice, sin—but then he points to how God's Son was born into these realities; and it is here that sweetness is found. Tasting and seeing God in reality is a process. Ignatius had to learn this himself through many painful experiences. At La Storta he received the grace to be placed with the Son bearing the Cross; and so he and his companions were drawn into the Son's pattern of life, with its joys and with its sufferings.

7. Similarly today the Society, in carrying out its mission, experiences the companionship of the Lord and the challenge of the Cross.[12] Commitment to 'the service of faith and the promotion of justice',[13] to dialogue with cultures and religions,[14] takes Jesuits to limit situations where they encounter energy and new life, but also anguish and death—where the 'divinity hides itself'.[15] The experience of a hidden God cannot always be avoided, but even in the depths of darkness when God seems concealed, the transforming light of God is able to shine. God labours intensely in this hiddenness. Rising from the tombs of personal life and history, the Lord appears when

[10] Exx, 124.

[11] Exx, 101–109.

[12] Exx, 53.

[13] GC 32, decree 2, n. 9.

[14] GC 34, decree 2, nn. 19–21.

[15] Exx, 196.

we least expect, with his personal consolation as a friend[16] and as the centre of a fraternal and servant community.[17] From this experience of God labouring in the heart of life, our identity as 'servants of Christ's mission'[18] rises up ever anew.

Our 'Way of Proceeding'

8. To find divine life at the depths of reality is a mission of hope given to us Jesuits. We travel again the path taken by Ignatius. As in his experience so too in ours; because a space of interiority is opened where God works in us, we are able to see the world as a place in which God is at work and which is full of his appeals and of his presence. Thus we enter, with Christ who offers living water,[19] into the dry and lifeless areas of the world. Our mode of proceeding is to trace the footprints of God everywhere, knowing that the Spirit of Christ is at work in all places and situations and in all activities and mediations that seek to make him more present in the world.[20] This mission of attempting 'to feel and to taste' (*sentir y gustar*) the presence and activity of God in all the persons and circumstances of the world places us Jesuits at the centre of a tension, pulling us both to God and to the world at the same time. Thus arises, for Jesuits on mission, a set of polarities, Ignatian in character, that accompanies our being firmly rooted in God at all times, while simultaneously being plunged into the heart of the world.

9. Being and doing; contemplation and action; prayer and prophetic living; being completely united with Christ

16 Exx, 224.

17 Matthew 18:20.

18 GC 34, decree 2.

19 Cf. John 4:10–15.

20 Cf. *Gaudium et spes*, 22; also GC 34, decree 6.

and completely inserted into the world with him as an apostolic body: all of these polarities mark deeply the life of a Jesuit and express both its essence and its possibilities.[21] The Gospels show Jesus in deep, loving relationship with his Father and, at the same time, completely given over to his mission among men and women. He is perpetually in motion: from God, for others. This is the Jesuit pattern too: with Christ on mission, ever contemplative, ever active. It is the grace—also the creative challenge—of our apostolic religious life that it must live this tension between prayer and action, between mysticism and service.

10. It is necessary for us to examine ourselves critically in order to remain mindful of the need to live faithfully this polarity of prayer and service.[22] However we cannot abandon this creative polarity, since it marks the essence of our lives as contemplatives in action, companions of Christ sent into the world.[23] In what we do in the world there must always be a transparency to God. Our lives must provoke the questions, 'who are you, that you do these things ... and that you do them in this way?' Jesuits must manifest—especially in the contemporary world of ceaseless noise and stimulation—a strong sense of the sacred inseparably joined to involvement in the world. Our deep love of God and our passion for his world should set us on fire—a fire that starts other fires! For ultimately there is no reality that is only profane for those who know how to look.[24] We must communicate this way of looking and provide a pedagogy, inspired by the Spiritual Exercises, that carries people—especially the

[21] Cf. Peter-Hans Kolvenbach, 'Sobre la vida religiosa', conference paper, Havana, Cuba, 1 June 2007, 1.

[22] Cf. Kolvenbach, 'Sobre la vida religiosa', 3.

[23] GC 33, GC 34.

[24] Cf. Pierre Teilhard de Chardin, *Le milieu divin* (London: Collins, 1960 [1957]), 66.

young—into it. Thus will they be able to see the world as St Ignatius did, as his life developed from what he understood at the Cardoner to the eventual founding of the Society with its mission to bring the message of Christ to the ends of the earth. This mission, with its roots in his experience, continues today.

A Life Shaped by the Vision of La Storta

11. St Ignatius had the most significant experience for the founding of the Society in the little chapel of La Storta, on his way to Rome. In this mystical grace he saw clearly 'that God the Father was puting him with Christ, his Son',[25] as the same Ignatius had asked insistently of Mary. At La Storta, the Father placed him with his Son carrying his Cross, and Jesus accepted him saying: 'I wish you to serve us'. Ignatius felt himself confirmed personally, and felt the group confirmed, in the plan moving their hearts to place themselves at the service of the Vicar of Christ on earth. 'Ignatius told me that God the Father imprinted these words on his heart: '*Ego ero vobis Romae propitius*''.[26] But this affirmation did not make Ignatius dream of easy paths, since he told his companions that they would encounter 'many things opposing them'[27] in Rome, and perhaps even be crucified. It is from Ignatius' encounter with the Lord at La Storta that the future life of service and mission of the companions emerges in its characteristic contours: following Christ bearing his Cross; fidelity to the Church and to the Vicar of Christ on earth; and living as friends of—and thus in—the Lord in one single apostolic body.

[25] *Autobiography*, 96.

[26] Diego Laínez, 'Adhortationes in librum Examinis' (1559), § 7 (MHSI 73, 133).

[27] *Autobiography*, 97.

Following Christ ...

12. To follow Christ bearing his Cross means opening ourselves with him to every thirst that afflicts humanity today. Christ is nourishment itself, the answer to every hunger and thirst. He is the bread of life, who, in feeding the hungry, draws them together and unites them.[28] He is the water of life,[29] the living water of which he spoke to the Samaritan woman in a dialogue that surprised his disciples because it took him, like free-flowing water, beyond the river banks of what was culturally and religiously familiar and into an exchange with someone with whom custom forbade him to speak at all. Jesus, in his outreach, embraced difference and new horizons. His ministry transcended boundaries. He invited his disciples to be aware of God's action in places and people they were inclined to avoid: Zacchaeus,[30] a Syro-Phoenician woman,[31] Roman centurions,[32] a repentant thief.[33] As water bringing life[34] to all who thirst, he showed himself interested in every parched area of the world; and in every parched area of the world he can thus be welcomed, for all who are thirsty can understand what living water means. This image of living water can give life to all Jesuits as servants of Christ in his mission because, having tasted this water themselves, they will be eager to offer it to anyone who thirsts and to reach out to people beyond frontiers—where water may not yet have welled up—to bring a new culture of dialogue to a rich, diverse and multifaceted world.

[28] Cf. Mark 6: 31–44.

[29] Cf. John 4: 7–15.

[30] Luke 19: 1–10.

[31] Mark 7: 24–30.

[32] Luke 7: 2–10; Mark 15: 39.

[33] Luke 23: 39–43.

[34] Cf. John 7: 38.

13. To follow Christ bearing his Cross means announcing his gospel of hope to the many poor who inhabit our world today. The world's many 'poverties' represent thirsts that, ultimately, only he who is living water can assuage. Working for his Reign will often mean meeting material needs, but it will always mean much more, because human beings thirst at many levels; and Christ's mission is directed to human beings. Faith and justice; it is never one without the other. Human beings need food, shelter, love, relationship, truth, meaning, promise, hope. Human beings need a future in which they can take hold of their full dignity; indeed they need an absolute future, a 'great hope' that exceeds every particular hope.[35] All of these things are already present in the heart of Christ's mission, which, as was particularly evident in his healing ministry, was always more than physical. In healing the leper, Jesus restored him to the community, gave him a sense of belonging. Our mission finds its inspiration in this ministry of Jesus. Following Jesus, we feel ourselves called not only to bring direct help to people in distress, but also to restore entire human persons in their integrity, reintegrating them in community and reconciling them with God. This frequently calls for an engagement that is long term, be it in the education of youth, in the spiritual accompaniment of the Exercises, in intellectual research, or in the service of refugees. But it is here, aided by grace and drawing on whatever professional capacities we may have that we try to offer ourselves to God fully, for his service.

14. The Son's way of acting provides the pattern for how we must act in the service of his mission.[36] Jesus preached the Reign of God; indeed it was given with his

[35] Benedict XVI, *Spe salvi* (30 November 2007), see §§ 4 and 35, for example.

[36] Exx, 91–98.

very presence.[37] And he showed himself as having come into the world not to do his own will but the will of his Father in heaven. Jesus' entire life was a *kenosis*, and he approached situations by self-forgetfulness, seeking not to be served, but to serve, and to give his life as a ransom for many.[38] Thus incarnation and paschal mystery unfold in his life-pattern; his life-pattern will be ours also when we join with him. As companions with him on mission, his way is our way.

15. In following this way Jesuits today affirm all that has been specified regarding the Society's mission in the last three General Congregations. The service of faith and the promotion of justice, indissolubly united, remain at the heart of our mission. This option changed the face of the Society. We embrace it again and we remember with gratitude our martyrs and the poor who have nourished us evangelically in our own identity as followers of Jesus: 'our service, especially among the poor, has deepened our life of faith, both individually and as a body'.[39] As followers of Jesus today, we reach out also to people who differ from us in culture and religion, aware that dialogue with them is integral also to our service of Christ's mission.[40] In every mission that we carry out, we seek only to be where he sends us. The grace we receive as Jesuits is to be and to go with him, looking on the world with his eyes, loving it with his heart, and entering into its depths with his unlimited compassion.

[37] Cf. Matthew 12:28; Luke 11:20, 17:21.

[38] Mark 10:45.

[39] GC 34, decree 2, n. 1.

[40] GC 34, decree 2.

In the Church and for the World ...

16. Knowing ourselves to be sent with Jesus as companions consecrated to him in poverty, chastity and obedience, although we are sinners, we listen attentively to the needs of people whom we seek to serve. We have been chosen to live as his companions in a single body governed by means of the account of conscience and held together by obedience: men of and for the Church under obedience to the Supreme Pontiff and our Father General and duly appointed Superiors.[41] In all of this, our aim is to be ever available for the more universal good—indeed desiring always the *magis*, that which is truly better, for the greater glory of God.[42] It is this availability for the Church's universal mission that marks our Society in a particular way, makes sense of our special vow of obedience to the Pope, and makes us a single apostolic body dedicated to serving, in the Church, men and women everywhere.

17. It is in its obedience, above all, that the Society of Jesus should be distinct from other religious families. One need only recall the letter of St Ignatius, where he writes:

> We can tolerate other religious institutes outdoing us in fasting and in other austerities that they practise according to their Rule, but it is my desire, dear brothers, that those who serve the Lord our God in this Society be outstanding in the purity and perfection of their obedience, the renunciation of their will, and the abnegation of their judgment.[43]

[41] Cf. Exx, 352–370.

[42] Cf. Exx, 23; *Constitutions*, VII. 2. D. [622].

[43] Letter to the Jesuits of Portugal (26 March 1553), §2 (MHSI 29, 671). English translation in Ignatius of Loyola, *Letters and Instructions* (St Louis: Institute of Jesuit Sources, 2006), 413.

It is to the obedience of the *Suscipe* that St Ignatius looked in order to highlight what it was that gave the Society its distinctive difference.

As an Apostolic Religious Community ...

18. Together with obedience, our Jesuit vows of poverty and chastity enable us to be shaped in the Church into the image of Jesus himself,[44] they also make clear and visible our availability for God's call. This availability is expressed in a variety of ways, according to the particular vocation of each. Thus the Society of Jesus is enriched and blessed by the presence of brothers, spiritual coadjutors and professed fathers who together, as companions in one family—enlivened in particular by the presence of those in formation—serve the mission of Christ according to the graces given to each.[45] Thus we Jesuits live our consecrated lives in response to different graces. We minister sacramentally at the heart of the Church, celebrating the Eucharist and the other sacraments and preaching the word of God faithfully. We take this word to the very ends of the earth, seeking to share its riches with people everywhere.

19. The differentiation of roles and ministries of Jesuits finds its necessary complement in a life of companionship lived in community. Our life together testifies to our friendship in the Lord, a sharing of faith and life together, above all in the celebration of the Eucharist. Following Jesus together acts as a pointer to the disciples *en mouvement* with their Lord. Jesuit identity and Jesuit mission are linked by community; indeed, identity, community and mission are a kind of tryptich shedding light on how our companionship is best understood. This

[44] 2 Corinthians 3:18.

[45] *Constitutions*, V.1.A. [511].

companionship shows how people different in background and diverse in talent can live together as true 'friends in the Lord'. Jesuit identity is relational; it grows in and through our diversities of culture, nationalities, and languages, enriching and challenging us. This is a process that we enter upon as we join the Society, and we grow in it every day. As we do so, our community life can become attractive to people, inviting them—above all the young—to 'come and see',[46] to join us in our vocation and to serve with us in Christ's mission. Nothing could be more desirable and more urgent today, since the heart of Christ burns with love for this world, with all its troubles, and seeks companions who can serve it with him.

A New Context—to New Frontiers

20. Serving Christ's mission today means paying special attention to its global context. This context requires us to act as a universal body with a universal mission, realising at the same time the radical diversity of our situations. It is as a worldwide community—and, simultaneously, as a network of local communities—that we seek to serve others across the world. Our mission of faith and justice, dialogue of religions and cultures, has acquired dimensions that no longer allow us to conceive of the world as composed of separate entities; we must see it as a unified whole in which we depend upon one another. Globalisation, technology and environmental concerns have challenged our traditional boundaries and have enhanced our awareness that we bear a common responsibility for the welfare of the entire world and its development in a sustainable and living-giving way.[47]

[46] John 1:39.

[47] Cf. *Globalisation and Marginalisation* (Rome: Social Justice Secretariat, 2006), 16–17.

21. Today's consumerist cultures do not foster passion and zeal but rather addiction and compulsion. They demand resistance. A compassionate response to these cultural malaises will be necessary and unavoidable if we are to share in the lives of our contemporaries. In such changing circumstances, our responsibility as Jesuits to collaborate at multiple levels has become an imperative. Thus our Provinces must work ever more together. So also must we work with others: religious men and women of other communities; lay persons; members of ecclesial movements; people who share our values but not our beliefs; in short, all people of good will.

22. God has created a world with diverse inhabitants, and this is good. Creation expresses the rich beauty of this lovable world: people working, laughing and thriving together[48] are signs that God is alive among us. However, diversity becomes problematic when the differences between people are lived in such a way that some prosper at the expense of others who are excluded, in such a way that people fight, killing each other, and are intent on destruction.[49] Then God in Christ suffers in and with the world, which he wants to renew. Precisely here is our mission situated. It is here that we must discern our mission according to the criteria of the *magis*[50] and the more universal good.[51] God is present in the darkness of life intent on making all things new. God needs collaborators in this endeavour: people whose grace consists in being received under the banner of his Son.[52] 'Nations' beyond geographical definitions await us, 'nations' that today include those who are poor and displaced, those who are

[48] Cf. Exx, 106.

[49] Cf. Exx, 108.

[50] Exx, 97.

[51] *Constitutions*, VII. 2. D. [622].

[52] Exx, 147.

profoundly lonely, those who ignore God's existence and those who use God as an instrument for political purposes. There are new 'nations', and we have been sent to them.[53]

23. Recalling Fr Jerónimo Nadal, we can say with him: 'the world is our house'.[54] As Fr Kolvenbach said recently:

> ... a stable monastery does not serve us, because we have received the entire world to tell about the good news ... we do not close ourselves up in the cloister, but we remain in the world amid the multitude of men and women that the Lord loves, since they are in the world.[55]

All men and women are our concern for dialogue and for proclamation because our mission is that of the Church: to discover Jesus Christ where we have not noticed him before and to reveal him where he has not been seen before. In other words, we look to 'find God in all things', following what St Ignatius proposes to us in the Contemplation to Attain Love.[56] The entire world becomes the object of our interest and concern.

24. Thus as this world changes, so does the context of our mission; and new frontiers beckon that we must be willing to embrace. So we plunge ourselves more deeply into that dialogue with religions that may show us that the Holy Spirit is at work all over the world that God loves. We turn also to the 'frontier' of the earth, increasingly degraded and plundered. Here, with passion for environ-

[53] Adolfo Nicolás, homily, Mass of Thanksgiving, 20 January 2008 (see below, 175–178).

[54] Jerónimo Nadal, '13ª Exhortatio complutensis' (Alcalá, 1561), §256 (MHSI 90, 469–470).

[55] Peter-Hans Kolvenbach, homily, *Regimini militantis ecclesiae*, celebrating the anniversary of the approval of the Society of Jesus, 27 September 2007.

[56] Cf. Exx, 230–237.

mental justice, we shall meet once again the Spirit of God seeking to liberate a suffering creation, which demands of us space to live and breathe.

Ite inflammate omnia

25. Legend has it that St Ignatius, when he sent St Francis Xavier to the East, told him: 'go, set the world alight'. With the birth of the Society of Jesus, a new fire was lit in a changing world. A novel form of religious life came about, not through human enterprise but as a divine initiative. The fire that was set alight then continues to burn in our Jesuit life today, as was said about St Alberto Hurtado, 'a fire that kindles other fires'. With it, we are called to set all things alight with the love of God.[57]

26. There are new challenges to this vocation today. We live our identity as companions of Jesus in a context where multiple images, the innumerable faces of a fragmented culture, compete for our attention. They seep into us, take root in the fertile soil of our natural desires, and fill us with sensations that flow through and take control of our feelings and decisions without our awareness. But we know and proclaim one image, Jesus Christ, true image of God and true image of humanity, who, when we contemplate him, becomes flesh in us, healing our inner brokenness, and making us whole as persons, as communities, and as an apostolic body dedicated to Christ's mission.

27. To live this mission in our broken world, we need fraternal and joyful communities in which we nourish and express with great intensity the sole passion that can unify our differences and bring to life our creativity. This passion grows out of our ever new experience of the Lord, whose

[57] Luke 12: 49.

imagination and love for our world are inexhaustible. This love invites us to,

> … participation in the mission of the One sent by the Father, in the Spirit, in an ever greater service, in love, with all the variants of the Cross, in an imitation and following of that Jesus who wants to lead all people and all of creation back to the glory of the Father.[58]

[58] Pedro Arrupe, 'Trinitarian Inspiration of the Ignatian Charism', §79, *AR,* 18/1 (1980), 150.

DECREE 3: Challenges to Our Mission Today: Sent to the Frontiers

I. Reaffirming Our Mission

1. As servants of Christ's mission, we recall with gratitude the graces received from the Lord during the past years. In our lives together as Jesuits, we have experienced an ongoing process of renewal and adaptation of our mission and way of proceeding as called for by the Second Vatican Council.[1]

2. Since the Council, the Spirit has led the whole Society gathered in General Congregations to the firm conviction that:

> The aim of our mission received from Christ, as presented in the Formula of the Institute, is the service of faith. The integrating principle of our mission is the inseparable link between faith and the promotion of the justice of the Kingdom.[2]

3. Reflecting on our experience during GC 34, we discerned that the service of faith in Jesus Christ and the promotion of the justice of the Kingdom preached by him can best be achieved in the contemporary world if inculturation and dialogue become essential elements of our way of proceeding in mission.[3] We experience this mission as being part of the Church's overall mission of evangelization, 'a single but complex reality' containing all these essential elements.[4] We want to reaffirm this mission which gives meaning to our religious apostolic life in the Church:

[1] Vatican II, *Perfectae caritatis*, 2.

[2] GC 34, decree 2, n. 14.

[3] GC 34, decree 2, nn. 14–21.

[4] Cf. John Paul II, *Redemptoris missio*, n. 41: 'Mission is a single but complex reality, and it develops in a variety of ways'. Cf. also nn. 52–54; 55–57.

Thus the aim of our mission (the service of faith) and its integrating principle (faith directed towards the justice of the Kingdom) are dynamically related to the inculturated proclamation of the gospel and dialogue with other religious traditions as integral dimensions of evangelization.[5]

4. During the past years, the fruitful engagement of the Society in the dialogue with people belonging to different cultures and religious traditions has enriched our service of faith and promotion of justice and confirmed that faith and justice cannot be simply one ministry among others; they are integral to all ministries and to our lives together as individuals, communities and a worldwide brotherhood.[6]

5. Our pastoral, educational, social, communication and spiritual ministries have increasingly found creative ways of implementing this mission in the challenging circumstances of the modern world. Different ministries carry out the mission in ways that are appropriate to them. However, all have experienced mission as the grace of being 'placed with the Son'. We remember with gratitude so many of our brothers and collaborators who have offered their lives generously in response to the call of the Lord to labour with him.

6. In our desire to continue 'serving the Lord alone and the Church, his spouse, under the Roman Pontiff',[7] we find confirmation in the words the Holy Father addressed to the members of this congregation:

Today, in the ecclesial and social context that marks the beginning of this millennium, I would like to

[5] GC 34, decree 2, n. 15.

[6] GC 32, decree 2, n. 9.

[7] Formula of the Institute, *Constitutions*, 1.

> encourage you and your confrères to continue on the path of this mission in full fidelity to your original charism. As my Predecessors have said to you on various occasions, the Church needs you, relies on you and continues to turn to you with trust ....[8]

7. In response to the challenging new contexts we face, we want to reflect further on our mission in the light of our experience.

II. A New Context for Mission

8. The new context in which we live our mission today is marked by profound changes, acute conflicts and new possibilities. In the words of the Holy Father:

> Your Congregation is being held during a period of great social, economic and political change; of conspicuous ethical, cultural and environmental problems, of conflicts of all kinds; yet also of more intense communication between peoples, of new possibilities for knowledge and dialogue, of profound aspirations for peace. These are situations that deeply challenge the Catholic Church and her capacity for proclaiming to our contemporaries the word of hope and salvation.[9]

9. We live in a global world. GC 34 already noted the 'growing consciousness of the interdependence of all people in one common heritage'.[10] This process has continued at a rapid pace; as a result, our interconnectedness has increased. Its impact has been felt deeply in all areas of our life, and it is sustained by interrelated cultural, social and political structures that affect the core of our mission of faith,

[8] Benedict XVI, allocution, § 2.

[9] Benedict XVI, allocution, § 2.

[10] GC 34, decree 3, n. 7.

justice, and all aspects of our dialogue with religion and culture.

10. Globalisation has also given birth to a world culture affecting all cultures; often this has resulted in a process of homogenisation and in policies of assimilation that deny the right of individuals and groups to live and to develop their own cultures. In the midst of this upheaval, post-modernism, mentioned also by GC 34,[11] has continued to shape the way the contemporary world and we Jesuits think and behave.

11. In this new world of instant communication and digital technology, of worldwide markets and of a universal aspiration for peace and well-being, we are faced with growing tensions and paradoxes: we live in a culture that shows partiality to autonomy and the present, and yet we have a world so much in need of building a future in solidarity; we have better ways of communication but often experience isolation and exclusion; some have greatly benefited, while others have been marginalised and excluded; our world is increasingly transnational, and yet it needs to affirm and protect local and particular identities; our scientific knowledge has reached the deepest mysteries of life, and yet the very dignity of life itself and the world we live in are threatened.

III. Call to Establish Right Relationships: A Mission of Reconciliation

12. In this global world, marked by such profound changes, we now want to deepen our understanding of the call to serve faith, promote justice and dialogue with culture and other religions in the light of the apostolic mandate to

[11] GC 34, decree 4, n. 19–24.

establish right relationships with God, with one another and with creation.[12]

13. In Luke's Gospel, Jesus inaugurated his public ministry in the synagogue of Nazareth.[13] Reading from the prophet Isaiah and acknowledging being anointed by the Spirit, he announced good news to the poor, the release of captives, the recovery of sight by the blind, and freedom for the oppressed. With this action he rooted himself and his ministry in the tradition of the Jewish prophets who passionately proclaimed God's justice, the duty of the people of Israel to establish right relationships with God, with one another (especially with the least among them) and with the land.[14]

14. In proclaiming God's message of love and compassion Jesus crossed over physical and socio-religious frontiers. His message of reconciliation was preached both to the people of Israel and to those living outside its physical and spiritual frontiers: tax collectors, prostitutes, sinners, and persons of all kinds who were marginalised and excluded. His ministry of reconciliation with God and with one another knew no boundaries. He spoke to the powerful, challenging them to a change of heart. He showed special love for the sinner, the poor widow and the lost sheep. The kingdom of God, which he constantly preached, became a vision for a world where all relationships are reconciled in God. Jesus confronted the powers that oppose this kingdom, and that opposition led him to death on the Cross, a death which he freely accepted in keeping with his mission. On the Cross we see all his words and actions revealed as expressions of the final reconciliation effected by the Crucified and Risen Lord,

[12] *Compendium of the Social Doctrine of the Church* (Dublin: Veritas, 2005), § 575.

[13] Luke 4: 16 ff.

[14] John Paul II, *Tertio millennio adveniente*, §§ 11–13.

through whom comes the new creation in which all relationships will be set right in God.[15]

15. Ignatius and his First Companions understood the importance of reaching out to people on the frontiers and at the centre of society, of reconciling those who were estranged in any way.[16] From the centre in Rome, Ignatius sent Jesuits to the frontiers, to the new world, 'to proclaim the Lord to peoples and cultures that did not yet know him'.[17] He sent Xavier to the Indies. Thousands of Jesuits followed, preaching the gospel to many cultures, sharing knowledge with, and learning from, others. He also wanted Jesuits to cross other types of frontiers between rich and poor, between educated and unlearned. He wrote a letter to the Jesuits at the Council of Trent on how to behave and insisted that they should minister to the sick. Jesuits opened colleges in Rome and in the great cities of Europe, and they taught children in villages across the world.

16. We are sent on mission by the Father, as were Ignatius and the First Companions at La Storta, together with Christ, risen and glorified but still carrying the Cross, as he labours in a world yet to experience the fullness of his reconciliation. In a world torn by violence, strife and division, we then are called with others to become instruments of God, who 'in Christ … was reconciling the world to himself, not counting their trespasses'.[18] This reconciliation calls us to build a new world of right relationships, a new Jubilee reaching across all divisions so that God might restore his justice for all.

[15] 2 Corinthians 5:19; Ephesians 2:16.

[16] Formula of the Institute, *Constitutions*, 1.

[17] Benedict XVI, allocution, § 3.

[18] 2 Corinthians 5:19.

17. This tradition of Jesuits building bridges across barriers becomes crucial in the context of today's world. We become able to bridge the divisions of a fragmented world only if we are united by the love of Christ our Lord, by personal bonds like those that linked Francis Xavier and Ignatius across the seas, and by the obedience that sends each one of us in mission to any part of this world.[19]

IV. Our Apostolic Response

18. As servants of Christ's mission we are invited to assist him as he sets right our relationships with God, with other human beings, and with creation. 'Our world is the theatre of a battle between good and evil', the Holy Father reminded us: and so we again place ourselves before the Lord in the meditation on the Two Standards.[20] There are powerful negative forces in the world, but we are also aware of God's presence permeating this world, inspiring persons of all cultures and religions to promote reconciliation and peace. The world where we work is one of sin and of grace.

Reconciliation with God

19. The Spiritual Exercises invite us to a renewed and deepened experience of reconciliation with God in Christ. We are called to share, with joy and respect, the grace of this experience that we have received and that nourishes our hope. Globalisation and new communication technologies have opened up our world and offer us new opportunities to announce with enthusiasm the good news of Jesus Christ and the Kingdom he proclaimed. Our ministries of the proclamation of the Word and the celebration of the life of Christ in the sacraments continue

[19] *Constitutions*, VIII. 1. 1–3. [655–659].

[20] Benedict XVI, allocution, § 6.

to be fundamental for our mission and our lives together as Jesuits. They must be seen as part of the three-fold responsibility that lies at the heart of the deepest nature of the Church: proclamation of the word of God (*kerygma-martyria*), celebrating the sacraments (*leitourgia*) and exercising the ministry of charity (*diakonia*).[21] In fulfilling this responsibility, we search for new forms of integral evangelization to 'reach the physical and spiritual places where others do not reach or have difficulty reaching',[22] always attentive to the demands of the cultural context within which we carry out our mission.

20. Globalisation has hastened the spread of a dominant culture which has brought to many people wide access to information and knowledge, an enhanced sense of the individual and freedom to choose, and openness to new ideas and values across the world. At the same time, this dominant culture has been marked by subjectivism, moral relativism, hedonism and practical materialism leading to 'an erroneous or superficial vision of God and man'.[23] In many societies people find themselves increasingly alone and struggling to find meaning for their lives. This has become a new apostolic challenge, and opportunity, for us. In all our ministries, we are called to a more serious engagement with this reality and to broaden the spaces of a continuing dialogue and reflection on the relationship between faith and reason, culture and morality, and faith and society, in order 'to make the Lord's true Face known to the many for whom he is still concealed or unrecognisable'.[24]

[21] *Deus caritas est*, 25.

[22] Benedict XVI, allocution, § 2.

[23] Benedict XVI, allocution, § 3.

[24] Benedict XVI, allocution, § 4.

21. The rapid pace of cultural change has been accompanied by an interior emptiness as well as a new interest in popular religiosity, a renewed search for meaning and a thirst for a spiritual experience often sought outside institutional religion. The Spiritual Exercises, which from the start have been a precious instrument in our hands, are today of invaluable assistance to many of our contemporaries. They help us to initiate and to progress in a life of prayer, to search for and to find God in all things, and to discern his will, making faith more personal and more incarnate. Our contemporaries are also helped in the difficult task of feeling a deeper sense of integration in their lives; the experience of the Exercises helps them achieve this by entering into a dialogue with God in freedom. We encourage Jesuits to give the Spiritual Exercises, 'to allow the Creator to deal immediately with the creature and the creature with its Creator and Lord',[25] to lead people to a deeper relationship with God in Christ and through that relationship to service of his Kingdom.

22. We live in a world of many religions and cultures. The erosion of traditional religious beliefs and the tendency to homogenize cultures has strengthened a variety of forms of religious fundamentalism. Faith in God is increasingly being used by some to divide people and communities, to create polarities and tensions which tear at the very fabric of our common social life. All these changes call us to the frontiers of culture and of religion. We need to strengthen and support those Jesuits and collaborators actively involved in the fourfold dialogue recommended by the Church,[26] to listen carefully to all, and to build bridges linking individuals and communities of goodwill.

[25] Exx, 15.

[26] See GC 34, decree 5, n. 4: dialogues of life, action, religious experience and theological exchange.

23. We need to discern carefully how we carry out educational and pastoral ministries, especially among youth, in this fast-changing postmodern culture. We need to walk with young people, learning from their generosity and compassion so as to help each other to grow through fragility and fragmentation to joyful integration of our lives with God and with others. Volunteer work with and for the poor helps young people to live in solidarity with others and find meaning in and direction for their lives.

24. Since Christ's death and resurrection has re-established our relationship with God, our service of faith must lead necessarily to the promotion of the justice of the Kingdom and to the care of God's creation.

Reconciliation with One Another

25. In this global world, there are social, economic and political forces that have facilitated the creation of new relationships among people, but there are other forces which have broken the bonds of love and solidarity within the human family. While many poor people have been lifted from poverty, the gap between rich and poor within nations and across national boundaries has increased. From the perspective of those living at the margins, globalisation appears to be a massive force that excludes and exploits the weak and the poor, which intensifies exclusion on the basis of religion, race, caste and gender.

26. A political consequence of globalisation has been the weakening of political sovereignty experienced by many nation-states all over the world. Some states feel this phenomenon as a particular type of global marginalisation and the loss of national respect. Transnational interests, unconstrained by national laws and often abetted by corruption, frequently exploit the natural resources of the poor. Powerful economic groups foment violence, war and arms trafficking.

27. Our commitment to help establish right relationships invites us to see the world from the perspective of the poor and the marginalised, learning from them, acting with and for them. In this context, the Holy Father reminds us that 'the preferential option for the poor is implicit in the Christological faith in a God who became poor for us, so as to enrich us with his poverty (cf. 2 Corinthians 8:9)'.[27] He invites us with a prophetic call to renew our mission 'among the poor and with the poor'.[28]

28. The complexity of the problems we face and the richness of the opportunities we are offered demand that we build bridges between rich and poor, establishing advocacy links of mutual support between those who hold political power and those who find it difficult to voice their interests. Our intellectual apostolate provides an inestimable help in constructing these bridges, offering us new ways of understanding in depth the mechanisms and links among our present problems. Many Jesuits in educational, social promotion and research institutions, together with others engaged directly with the poor, are already committed to this work. Still others have helped in the growth of corporate social responsibility, the creation of a more humane business culture, and economic development initiatives with the poor.

29. Among the defining characteristics of our globalised world are new communications technologies. They have a tremendous impact on all of us, especially the young. They can be powerful instruments for building and supporting international networks in our advocacy, in our work of education, and in our sharing of our spirituality and our faith. This Congregation urges Jesuit institutions to put

[27] Benedict XVI, allocution, § 8.

[28] Benedict XVI, allocution, § 8.

these new technologies at the service of those at the margins.

30. Our response to these situations must come from our deep faith in the Lord who calls us to work with others for the Kingdom of God, for the establishment of right relationships among people and with creation. In this way we cooperate with the Lord in building a new future in Christ for a 'globalisation in solidarity, a globalisation without marginalisation'.[29]

Reconciliation with Creation

31. Following the directive[30] of GC 34, Fr Peter-Hans Kolvenbach commissioned a study and invited all 'Jesuits and those who share our mission to show ever more effective ecological solidarity in our spiritual, communal and apostolic lives'.[31] This invitation calls us to move beyond doubts and indifference to take responsibility for our home, the earth.

32. Care of the environment affects the quality of our relationships with God, with other human beings and with creation itself. It touches the core of our faith in and love for God, 'from whom we come and towards whom we are journeying'.[32] It might be said that St Ignatius teaches us this care of the environment in the Principle and Foundation[33] when speaking of the goodness of creation, as

[29] John Paul II, 'From the Justice of Each Comes Peace for All', World Day of Peace message, 1 January 1998, § 3.

[30] GC 34, decree 20, n. 2.

[31] Peter-Hans Kolvenbach, 'Father General's Introduction', *Promotio Iustitiae*, 70 (April 1999), 9.

[32] Benedict XVI, 'The Human Family: A Community of Peace', World Day of Peace message, 1 January 2008, § 7.

[33] Exx, 23.

well as in the *Contemplatio ad amorem* when describing the active presence of God within creation.[34]

33. The drive to access and exploit sources of energy and other natural resources is very rapidly widening the damage to earth, air, water and our whole environment to the point that the future of our planet is threatened. Poisoned water, polluted air, massive deforestation, and deposits of atomic and toxic waste are causing death and untold suffering, particularly to the poor. Many poor communities have been displaced, and indigenous peoples have been the most affected.

34. In heeding the call to restore right relationships with creation, we have been moved anew by the cry of those suffering the consequences of environmental destruction, by the many postulates received, by the recent teaching of the Holy Father, and by the many episcopal conferences on this issue.

35. This Congregation urges all Jesuits and all partners engaged in the same mission, particularly the universities and research centres, to promote studies and practices focusing on the causes of poverty and the question of the environment's improvement. We should find ways in which our experiences with refugees and the displaced on one hand, and people who work for the protection of the environment on the other hand, could interact with those institutions, so that research results and advocacy have effective practical benefits for society and the environment. Advocacy and research should serve the poor and those who work for the protection of the environment. This ought to shed new light on the appeal of the Holy Father that costs should be justly shared 'taking due account of the different levels of development'.[35]

[34] Exx, 230–237.

[35] Benedict XVI, 'The Human Family', § 7.

36. In our preaching, teaching and retreat direction, we should invite all people to appreciate more deeply our covenant[36] with creation as central to right relationships with God and one another, and to act accordingly in terms of political responsibility, employment, family life and personal lifestyle.

V. Global Preferences

37. In continuity with the recommendations[37] made by GC 34, and to respond effectively to the global challenges described above, this Congregation has emphasized the importance of structures for apostolic planning, implementation and accountability at all levels of the Society's government.[38]

38. During the last years the Society has made a concerted and generous effort to increase inter-provincial cooperation in a variety of ways. In this context, GC 34 stated that 'Father General ... in his regular direct contacts with Provincials and with the Moderators of the Conferences, will discern the greater needs of the universal Church and will establish global and regional priorities'.[39]

39. While respecting provincial or regional priorities, these 'preferences' indicate apostolic areas requiring 'special or privileged attention'.[40] In our present context, we may confidently say that they offer areas for the realisation of

[36] Benedict XVI, 'The Human Family', §7.

[37] GC 34, decree 21.

[38] GC 35, decree 5, nn. 12, 18–21.

[39] GC 34, decree 21, n. 28.

[40] Peter-Hans Kolvenbach, 'Souhaits de noël et de nouvel an: nos préférences apostoliques' (1 January 2003), *AR*, 23/1 (2003), 31–36,. In English as 'Christmas and New Year Greetings: Our Apostolic Preferences', letter to all Major Superiors, 2003/01: 'The choice of apostolic priorities ... has been accomplished in prayerful discernment, identifying some of the most important and urgent needs, those that are most universal, or those to which the Society is being called to respond more generously'.

the mission orientations provided by this decree. In consultation with the Conferences of Major Superiors, Fr Peter-Hans Kolvenbach decided on the following apostolic preferences:

> (i) *Africa*. Aware of the cultural, social and economic differences in Africa and Madagascar, but also conscious of the great opportunities, challenges, and variety of Jesuit ministries, we acknowledge the Society's responsibility to present a more integral and human vision of this continent. In addition, all Jesuits are invited to greater solidarity with and effective support of the Society's mission of inculturating faith and promoting more justice in this continent.
>
> (ii) *China* has become of central importance not only for East Asia but for the whole of humanity. We want to continue our respectful dialogue with its people, aware that China is an important key for a peaceful world and has great potential for enriching our faith tradition, as many of its people long for a spiritual encounter with God in Christ.
>
> (iii) The *intellectual apostolate* has been a defining characteristic of the Society of Jesus from its beginning. Given the complex yet interrelated challenges that Jesuits face in every apostolic sector, GC 35 calls for a strengthening and renewal of this apostolate as a privileged means for the Society to respond adequately to the important intellectual contribution to which the Church calls us. Advanced studies for Jesuits must be encouraged and supported throughout formation.
>
> (iv) The *inter-provincial institutions in Rome* are a special mission of the Society received directly from the Holy Father.[41] Ignatius wrote that we should

[41] Benedict XVI, 'Address to the Pontifical Gregorian University' (3 November 2006), *AR*, 23/4 (2006), 696–697.

'treat the missions from His Holiness ... as being most important'.[42] This Congregation reaffirms the commitment of the Society to the Houses and Common Works of Rome as an apostolic preference of the universal Society. To serve that mission most fruitfully, there should be ongoing strategic planning and evaluation by the institutions and by the Society.[43]

(v) *Migration and refugees*. Ever since Fr Arrupe called the attention of the Society to the plight of refugees, the phenomenon of forced migration for different reasons has increased dramatically. These massive movements of people create great suffering among millions. Therefore, this Congregation reaffirms that attending to the needs of migrants, including refugees, internally displaced and trafficked people, continue to be an apostolic preference of the Society. Moreover, we reaffirm that the Jesuit Refugee Service adhere to its present Charter and Guidelines.

40. We invite Father General to continue to discern the preferences for the Society, to review the above preferences, to update their specific content, and to develop plans and programmes that can be monitored and evaluated.

VI. Conclusion

41. Our mission is not limited to our works. Our personal and community relationship with the Lord, our relationship to one another as friends in the Lord, our solidarity with the poor and marginalised, and a lifestyle responsible to creation are all important aspects of our lives as Jesuits. They authenticate what we proclaim and what we do in fulfilling our mission. The privileged place of this collective

[42] *Constitutions*, VII.1.1. [603].

[43] Cf. GC 34, decree 22.

witness is our life in community. Thus, Jesuit community is not just for mission: it is itself mission.[44]

42. An apostolic body that lives in creative obedience and in which the members know how to appreciate their collaborators in mission gives a powerful witness to the world. Our ministries and institutions are the first place where faith in our Lord Jesus Christ, which we profess, should be incarnated through the justice of our relationships with God, others and creation.

43. In this global context it is important to highlight the extraordinary potential we possess as an international and multicultural body. Acting consistently with this character can not only enhance the apostolic effectiveness of our work but in a fragmented and divided world it can witness to the reconciliation in solidarity of all the children of God.

[44] Cf. Peter-Hans Kolvenbach, 'Sur la vie communautaire' (12 March 1998), *AR*, 22/3 (1998), 276–289. In English as 'On Community Life', letter to the whole Society.

DECREE 4: Obedience in the Life of the Society of Jesus

Introduction

1. Obedience is central to the mission and union of the Society of Jesus and a special bond of obedience links the Society to the Holy Father, 'the successor of St Peter and Vicar of Christ on earth' as St Ignatius was accustomed to call him. Therefore, the Society must constantly deepen and renew its life of obedience. The last four General Congregations of the Society have not been silent on this theme, and the 35th General Congregation confirms their directives and norms.[1] In addition, we feel the need to add a word of encouragement and guidance adapted to our present circumstances and to respond to the request of Pope Benedict XVI that we reflect on the Fourth Vow.[2] To do so, we will begin, as the Second Vatican Council instructs us,[3] with a reflection on the sacred Scriptures and the charism of our Founder.

The Experience of St Ignatius and the First Companions

2. We find the origins of the mysticism of service of St Ignatius and his First Companions in their experience of the Spiritual Exercises. In the meditations of the First Week[4] they came into contact with the merciful love of God extended to them in Christ. Through the contemplations of the Second Week, and especially the invitation of the Eternal King,[5] they felt called 'to make offerings of greater moment ... offering their whole selves for this labour'.[6] In

[1] See *NC* 149–156, 252–262; GC 31, decree 17; GC 32, decree 11; GC 34, decree 11.

[2] Cf. Peter-Hans Kolvenbach, letter on the Pope's response to all Major Superiors and Electors of GC 35, 2007/03, 21 February 2007 (see below, 148–149).

[3] *Perfectae caritatis*, 2.

[4] Exx, 45–47.

[5] Exx, 91–100.

[6] Exx, 97, 96.

the Meditation on the Two Standards,[7] they asked to be placed under Christ's standard in order to 'put into practice their union with Christ and his power as a grace of the Spirit of the Lord'.[8] Each of them wanted to feel 'that he thinks with Christ's thoughts, wills with Christ's will, and remembers with Christ's memory; that he is and lives and acts no longer as himself but completely in Christ'.[9]

3. The First Companions' desire to accompany Christ and to wear themselves out in his service so that all men and women might be saved and freed from their suffering and slavery took on concrete form in the vow they took at Montmartre in 1534. If their plan to travel to the Holy Land did not come to fruition, they promised to place themselves at the disposal of the Pope so that he might use their help as he thought would be for God's glory and the salvation of souls.[10] This offering of the First Companions was confirmed in the vision at La Storta where, through St Ignatius, the Eternal Father gave them to his Son as his companions and promised to be propitious to them in Rome.[11] In this way, God responded to their unceasing prayer, through the intercession of the Virgin Mary, to be placed with the Son.

4. When the Pope decided to send the First Companions on various missions that would involve their separation from each other, they asked whether they should unite themselves as a body. According to the Deliberation of the First Fathers, they unanimously decided, after prayerful discernment, to become a body in

[7] Exx, 136.

[8] Jerónimo Nadal, 'Orationis observationes', edited by Michael Nicolau (MHSI 90a, 122), §308.

[9] Nadal, 'Orationis observationes', §308.

[10] *Autobiography*, 85.

[11] *Autobiography*, 96; Jerónimo Nadal, 'Exhortationes in Hispania' (1554), §16 (MHSI 66, 313); Laínez, 'Adhortationes in librum Examinis', §7 (MHSI 73, 133).

which each would care for the others, strengthening their bond of union through mutual knowledge and sharing in each others' lives.[12]

5. Before their priestly ordination in 1537, the First Companions had taken vows of poverty and chastity. In 1539 they asked whether or not to take a vow of obedience to one of the group at the same time that they dedicated their entire will, understanding and strength to carrying out the missions they received from the Pope. Their answer to this question was also affirmative. After prayerful discernment, they concluded that vowing obedience to one of them would allow them 'to follow the will of God in all things with greater certainty and with greater praise and merit'.[13]

6. The papal bull *Regimini militantis Ecclesiae* is the Church's confirmation of this foundational experience. That is why the only way the Society can be true to the historical and mystical experience of the First Companions is 'to serve the Lord alone and the Church, his spouse, under the Roman Pontiff, the Vicar of Christ on earth'.[14]

7. The goal of the spiritual formation outlined in the *Constitutions* is to prepare Jesuits in formation for apostolic life in the Society and to deepen the apostolic life of the body of the Society on mission. The Third Part of the *Constitutions* introduces the novice to spiritual and apostolic discernment. It confronts him with the demands of a life lived in companionship at the service of the apostolate and offers him an opportunity to grow in faith and trust in the Lord, to understand the obstacles to

[12] Deliberation of the First Fathers (1539), § 3 (MHSI 63, 3–4).

[13] Deliberation, § 4 (MHSI 63, 4).

[14] Formula of the Institute, *Constitutions*, 1.

human and spiritual growth, and to avail himself of the spiritual means to overcome them.[15]

8. The Sixth and Seventh Parts of the *Constitutions* address formed Jesuits and propose the fundamental virtues of apostolic life in the Society: *discreta caritas* and the *magis*.[16] The Sixth Part insists that passionate love for Christ must become incarnate in obedience to the Pope and Superiors in the Society whose commands the formed Jesuit should obey as if they come from Christ because it is for love of Christ that he obeys.[17] The whole Seventh Part is a demonstration of the foundational principle of obedience, the *magis.* Here the emphasis is on discernment, freedom and creativity in seeking the will of God and engaging in apostolic activity.[18] Thus, fidelity to obedience becomes the way the Jesuit incarnates the values of the gospel and of the Spiritual Exercises: availability for being at the service of the Kingdom of God and freedom to be a 'man for others'.

Theological Aspects of Obedience

9. Before all else, our obedience seeks to fulfil the will of God. Its foundation is personal love for Jesus Christ, who has deigned to choose us as his companions. The Holy Spirit, who has freely poured this love into our hearts, inspires in us a desire to identify ourselves with Christ and gives us the strength to 'let the same mind be in you that

[15] *Constitutions,* III.1.10. [260]; *NC,* 45, §1; GC 32, decree 6, n. 7.

[16] *Constitutions,* VI.3.1. [582].

[17] *Constitutions,* VI.1.1. [547], VI.1.2. [551].

[18] Ignatius' instruction to the Jesuit sent to be patriarch of Ethiopia breathes the atmosphere of the Seventh Part. 'All this is proposed under the heading of advice. The patriarch should not consider himself obliged to comply with it. Rather, he should be guided by *discreta caritas*, taking into account the circumstances of the moment and the unction of the Holy Spirit which should be his principal guide in everything.' (MHSI 36, 689–690)

was in Christ Jesus'.[19] This desire 'to clothe ourselves with the same garb and uniform of [the] Lord'[20] situates us in the mysticism of the Third Degree of Humility.[21]

10. Our religious vows place us with the Lord and move us to follow him in fidelity to the mission of announcing the Kingdom conferred on him by the Father. From the first moment of his existence, Jesus' life was orientated to the Father: 'See, God, I have come to do your will'.[22] Jesus has no other food but the will of the Father.[23] Knowing himself sent by the Father 'that all who see the Son and believe in him may have eternal life',[24] Jesus does not act of himself but only does 'what he sees the Father doing'.[25]

11. Jesus' fidelity to his mission brought him into conflict with human sinfulness and injustice, and it led him to 'death—even death on a cross'.[26] Conquering even his resistance and weakness, 'Abba ... not what I want, but what you want',[27] Jesus became the source of salvation for all by fulfilling the Father's will. 'Although he was Son he learned obedience through suffering and having been made perfect became the source of eternal salvation for all who obey him.'[28]

12. To be joined with Christ as his companions in obedience to the will of the Father allows us to become servants of his mission of evangelization. Obedience frees us to give ourselves exclusively to the service of the

[19] Philippians 2: 5.

[20] *Constitutions*, General Examen 4. 44. [101].

[21] Exx, 167.

[22] Hebrews 10: 7.

[23] John 4: 34.

[24] John 6: 40.

[25] John 5:19.

[26] Philippians 2: 8.

[27] Mark 14: 36.

[28] Hebrews 5: 9.

gospel. By freeing us from our own 'self-love, self-will, and self-interests',[29] obedience lets us dedicate ourselves totally to what God loves and to those who are the object of God's special concern.

13. To be joined to Christ as his companions in obedience and in mission, in poverty and in chastity, makes us witnesses to the Kingdom and its values.[30] At the same time that we work for the growth of the Kingdom in this world, we await its fullness as a gift God alone can give. Renouncing the use of this world's goods as if they were our own, and putting our affections and our entire freedom at the service of the Kingdom, we contribute to making the Kingdom we long for a reality here and now.

14. The incarnation of the Son of God in human history invites us to see God in all things and leads us to understand that he can make use of all things in carrying out his saving work. This is why our discernment must take into account our historical, social and personal circumstances; it is in the midst of them that God calls us to fulfil His will.

15. When created realities have been distorted by sin and injustice, however, they can cease to express the goodness of God and can become impediments to our response to the Lord's call. This is why some degree of participation in Jesus' *kenosis*[31] will never be absent from our lives. Like Jesus, we spend ourselves day after day, trustfully handing ourselves over to the will of God who has shown us so many proofs of his love, even though at

[29] Exx, 189.

[30] Vatican II, *Lumen gentium*, 44.

[31] Philippians 2: 5–8.

times he may seem far from us[32] or hidden from us by the effects of sin.[33]

16. By his resurrection, the Lord continues to be present in the Church through the Spirit, and through the Church he continues to make his voice heard. 'Whoever listens to you listens to me, and whoever rejects you rejects me.'[34] The Church is the mediation of the Word of God and the sacrament of our salvation, in spite of the imperfections of her children. It is through the Church that the Christian finds God, and we profess obedience in the Church in order to serve God. Within the Church, the Society is a privileged place where the will of God is manifested to us; it becomes our 'pathway to God'.[35]

17. We will only be able to live our vow of obedience as freedom and true self-realisation if the mystical experience of passionate love for Christ, the one who is sent by the Father and who is obedient to the Father's will, remains alive in us and if we daily renew our unconditional commitment to be his companions. It is precisely our love for Jesus Christ that will make our work in service to his mission fruitful, because,

> ... the means which unite the human instrument with God and so dispose it that it may be wielded well by his divine hand are more effective than those which equip it in relation to human beings.[36]

[32] Matthew 27:46; Mark 15:34.

[33] Exx, 196.

[34] Luke 10:16.

[35] Formula of the Institute, *Constitutions*, 1.

[36] *Constitutions*, X.1. [813].

Our Contemporary Context and its Challenges

18. Many positive values prized by our contemporaries are essential to living religious obedience according to our Jesuit way of proceeding: respect for the human person and for human rights, willingness to engage in dialogue marked by freedom of expression, openness to creative alternatives, the desire to build community, and the longing to live for something greater than oneself. But our culture is also marked by a tendency to exaggerated self-sufficiency and individualism that create difficulties for the practice of religious obedience.

19. Faith in Jesus Christ teaches us that self-realisation comes from self-giving and that freedom is not so much the power to choose as the power to order our choices towards love. At the same time, love for Jesus Christ and the desire to follow him call us to trusting commitment. Commitment to the Word Incarnate cannot be separated from commitment to the concrete mediations of the Word that are at the centre of our lives, the Church and the Society which exists to serve the Church. At times, however, our desire to commit ourselves to the Lord in personal trust is not matched by our desire to commit ourselves to the Church or to the body of the Society and its way of proceeding.

20. An exaggerated desire for autonomy has led some to various expressions of self-sufficiency and lack of commitment: lack of availability to our Superiors, lack of prudence in the expression of our opinions, lack of a spirit of cooperation in our approach to the local Church, and even disaffection from the Church and the Society. Some have used the language of discernment to excuse a desire to determine their own mission, forgetting that discernment in the Society is a communal exercise that takes into account a multiplicity of voices but reaches its completion only in the conferral of a mission by the Superior.

21. The patterns of our contemporary world have their effect on the exercise of authority as well. The way in which our world prizes productivity can lead to overwork, and this can lead to distraction and lack of attention to the human person. The exercise of authority can be reduced to an exercise of power that marginalises others or to a demand to be heard that is not matched by sufficient willingness to listen. We know these tendencies disfigure many structures and relationships in our world; we cannot imagine we will be immune from their influence when obedience places us in positions of authority within the Society or in institutions through which the Society carries out its mission.

22. These attitudes exist around us and within us. However, many of them are far from the spirit of the gospel, far from the spirit of obedience the Society wishes to foster in its members, and far from the ideal of obedience our way of proceeding presupposes.

Some Specific Aspects of the Practice of Obedience in the Society

23. The practice of obedience in the Society has its roots in the spiritual experience of Ignatius and the First Companions. Drawn together by the Spiritual Exercises, they came to have but one goal: to be sent on mission in the image of the Son and so serve the Lord in companionship. Therefore, obedience in the Society is grounded in the desire to be sent effectively, to serve completely, and to create ever stronger bonds of union among ourselves.[37]

24. These three strands come together in the account of conscience. For this reason, the account of conscience is

[37] *NC*, 149–156.

essential to the practice of obedience in the Society.[38] A Jesuit reveals to his Superior all that is happening in his soul, the graces that he has received and the temptations he has undergone, so that his Superior can more prudently and confidently send him on mission. The account is repeated annually so that the Jesuit and his Superior can evaluate and confirm that mission together.

25. This degree of transparency is possible because our Superiors are also our companions. Ignatius wanted Superiors to love their companions. To love is to act responsibly. Jesuits bear the responsibility to reveal themselves completely to their Superiors; Superiors bear the responsibility to hear their brothers attentively and to dialogue with them honestly. This is especially true when a Jesuit humbly represents to his Superior any difficulty he has with the mission he has been given, a practice Ignatius valued and encouraged.[39]

26. The trust that marks obedience is mutual. Jesuits make an act of trust in their Superiors when they obey; Superiors make an act of trust in their brothers when they send them on mission. This trust is grounded in the Superior's appreciation of the Jesuit he sends as someone who discerns; that is, someone who seeks familiarity with the Lord through prayer, desires freedom from disordered attachment, and thus opens himself to the guidance of the Spirit in an ongoing quest to discover the divine will.

27. Because Ignatius knew and trusted the prayerful desires of the Jesuits he sent on mission, he left much to their discretion.[40] Following the example of Ignatius, the Society expects that Jesuits will exercise creativity in carrying out their mission as they see circumstances

[38] *NC*, 155, §1.

[39] *Constitutions*, V. 4. F. [543], VII. 2. I. [627].

[40] *Constitutions*, VII. 3. 1. [633]–VII. 3. A. [635].

require, that they will go beyond what has been asked in the true spirit of the *magis*.[41] Thus the Superior's trust expresses itself in effective delegation, and the Jesuit who obeys knows he can rely on his Superior's openness to creative initiatives he might propose.[42] This is why obedience in the Society has rightly been described as an exercise of creative fidelity.[43] It is creative, because it calls on the individual's freedom and resourcefulness. It is fidelity because it calls for a generous response to the directives of the Superior whose duty it is to make decisions 'looking to the purpose of the Constitutions, which is the greater divine service and the good of those who live in this Institute'.[44]

28. A consideration of the practice of obedience would be incomplete if it were limited to the relationship between the Superior and the individual Jesuit. The community has its role to play. We obey our Superiors in community so that our common life can effectively support our mission and become a sign of the possibility of human communion our world so sorely needs.[45] The community is also a privileged place for the practice of apostolic discernment, whether through formally structured communal discernment[46] or through informal conversation that has the more effective pursuit of the mission as its goal. Such discernment will help us not only accept our

[41] *Constitutions*, VII. 2. D. [622]–VII. 2. E. [623].

[42] GC 31, decree 17, n. 11.

[43] All of this clarifies the significance of phrases like 'an old man's staff' or '*perinde ac cadaver*' that can be found in the *Constitutions*. The context makes it clear that to obey is not to become lifeless; rather, it is to offer oneself to be carried by the mission conferred by the Superior. 'For in this way the obedient man ought joyfully to employ himself in any task in which the Superior desires to employ him in aid of the whole body of the religious order.' (*Constitutions*, VI. 1. 1. [547])

[44] *Constitutions*, IX. 3. 8. [746].

[45] Kolvenbach, 'Sur la vie communautaire'.

[46] *NC*, 150–151.

personal missions but also rejoice in and support the missions received by our brothers. In this way, our common mission is strengthened and the union of minds and hearts confirmed and deepened.

29. For Ignatius, and for the Jesuit, obedience is both grace and gift. It is a path to which we are called by the Lord, and it is the Lord who enables us to follow this path in his service. A personal history of generous response to the grace of obedience allows a Jesuit to serve joyfully and effectively.

The Fourth Vow of Obedience to the Pope with Regard to Missions

30. Ignatius and the First Companions offered themselves to the Vicar of Christ to be sent on mission out of a 'desire to serve the Church in the most beneficial way possible'.[47] By means of the Fourth Vow pronounced by the professed, the whole body of the Society puts itself at the disposition of the ministry of the Successor of Peter for 'distribution into the vineyard of Christ our Lord'.[48] In this way, we achieve greater availability to the divine will and offer the Church better service.

31. The Fourth Vow, which Ignatius himself defined as 'our beginning and principal foundation',[49] expresses what is specific to the Society: total availability to serve the Church wherever the Pope sends us. The Fourth Vow also makes clear the place of the Society in the Church. It gives the Society structural incorporation into the life of the Church by linking its charism as an apostolic religious

[47] Benedict XVI, 'Allocution to the Members of the Society of Jesus' (22 April 2006), *AR* 23/4 (2006), 677.

[48] *Constitutions*, VII.1.A. [604].

[49] 'Declarationes circa missiones' (1544–1545) (MHSI 63, 162); Pierre Favre, *Memoriale*, n.18 (MHSI 68, 498); GC 31, decree 1, n.4.

order to the hierarchical structure of the Church in the person of the Pope. It is through this vow that the Society participates in the universal mission of the Church and that the universality of its mission, carried out through a wide range of ministries in the service of local churches, is guaranteed.

32. According to the *Constitutions*, 'the entire purport of this Fourth Vow of obedience to the Pope was and is with regard to missions ... for having the members dispersed throughout the various parts of the world'.[50] This is the matter of the vow. But the *Constitutions* also invite us to distinguish ourselves in obedience 'not only in the matters of obligation but also in others, even though nothing else be perceived except an indication of the Superior's will without an expressed command'.[51] This is thoroughly congruent with Ignatius' ideal of obedience, which holds 'that obedience is imperfect in which there does not exist, in addition to the execution, ... agreement in willing and judging between him who commands and him who obeys'.[52]

33. The availability promised in the Fourth Vow is distinct from the Ignatian spirituality of 'the proper attitude we ought to have in the Church' or '*sentire cum Ecclesia*'.[53] However, both are rooted in the love we have for Christ our Lord, a love that extends itself to love for the Church and for 'the one who holds the place of Christ

[50] *Constitutions*, V.3.C. [529] and VII.1.B. [605].

[51] *Constitutions*, VI.1.1. [547]. Although the reference in the *Constitutions* is to obedience to Jesuit Superiors, the 31st General Congregation applies the citation to obedience to the Pope. 'With all our force and energy we should strive to obey first the Sovereign Pontiff and then the Superiors of the Society "not only in matters of obligation, but also in others, even at the mere hint of the Superior's will, apart from any express command".' (GC 31, decree 17, n. 10)

[52] *Constitutions*, VI.1.C. [550].

[53] Exx, 352. Cf. GC 34, decree 11, and 'Final Allocution of Fr Kolvenbach to the 69th Congregation of Procurators' (Loyola, 23 September 2003), *AR*, 23/1 (2003), 431–438.

our Lord for us'.[54] This is why we speak of being united with the Pope effectively and affectively. Taken together, the Fourth Vow and our ecclesial spirituality move us to offer the service asked of us by the Pope.[55]

34. The Society is deeply grateful to God for its vocation to serve the Church and derives great consolation from the innumerable examples of generous Jesuits who offer their lives in service to the mission of Christ throughout the world, making themselves available for missions from the Holy Father and collaborating with local churches under the guidance of their pastors. In the name of the whole Society, the 35th General Congregation asks the Lord's pardon for those times when its members have been lacking in love, discretion or faithfulness in their service of the Church. At the same time, this Congregation affirms the Society's commitment to grow daily in love for the Church and availability to the Pope.

Obedience in Daily Life

35. This Congregation does not want to repeat everything set down about obedience in the *Constitutions* and *Complementary Norms*; neither does it want to repeat the directives on obedience to be found in the decrees of the most recent General Congregations. However, we do wish to offer some advice that can assist us in our present circumstances so that we can continue to distinguish ourselves in the perfection of our obedience[56] as St Ignatius urges us.

[54] *Constitutions*, VI.1.3. [552].

[55] *NC*, 253.

[56] 'We can tolerate other religious institutes outdoing us in fasting and in other austerities that they practise according to their Rule, but it is my desire, dear brothers, that those who serve the Lord our God in this Society be outstanding in the purity and perfection of their obedience, the renunciation of their will, and the abnegation of their judgment.' (Ignatius, 'Letter to the Jesuits of Portugal' [MHSI

Jesuits in Formation

36. The 35th General Congregation invites Jesuits in formation to live their progressive incorporation into the Society with joyful hearts, reproducing the First Companions' fruitful experience of being friends in the Lord and committing their lives to generous service of all men and women, especially those most in need.

37. We encourage Jesuits in formation to grow throughout the stages of formation in the spirituality of obedience and in availability for placing their lives and freedom at the service of the mission of Christ. It will be good for them to take advantage of the opportunities for self-abnegation that community life, constant and rigorous dedication to studies and other aspects of their experience will doubtless provide. Self-abnegation, 'the fruit of our joy at the approach of the Kingdom and [the result of] a progressive identification with Christ',[57] is a virtue Jesuits need to accept peacefully the sometimes difficult demands of obedience.

38. We encourage *formatores* to help Jesuits in formation understand and live the mystical source of obedience: an unconditional love for the Lord which will bring them to a desire to serve him in fulfilling the Father's will. We ask *formatores* to help Jesuits in formation become progressively aware of the demands of a life of obedience: transparency with Superiors, esteem for the account of conscience, the responsible exercise of personal initiative, and a spirit of discernment which accepts the decisions of the Superior with good grace.

29, 671])

[57] *NC*, 223 § 4.

39. The spirituality and tradition of the Society require that Jesuits be filled with a spirit of obedience to the Holy Father as an essential characteristic of our mission and identity. Jesuit spiritual and ecclesial formation should emphasize availability for mission and 'the proper attitude we ought to have in the Church' as established by the 34th General Congregation.[58]

Formed Jesuits

40. The 35th General Congregation invites formed Jesuits to grow in interior freedom and trust in God. In this way, their availability to go to any part of the world and undertake any ministry of more universal scope and from which greater fruit can be expected will increase.[59]

41. The Congregation encourages all Jesuits to strengthen their affection for the Pope and their respect for the pastors of the Church and to correct any faults that might exist in this regard.

42. Similarly, the Congregation asks all Jesuits to recognise with gratitude the service that Local and Major Superiors offer the Society and to support them in their task.

43. It is of vital importance that all Jesuits consider the account of conscience essential for the practice of obedience and that they offer it according to the guidelines set down by Fr Kolvenbach in his letter to the Society of 21 February 2005. Because 'the mission is conferred, confirmed, or changed'[60] in the account of conscience, it should be given in the first place to the Major Superior. However, what the letter says in regard to

[58] GC 34, decree 11.

[59] *Constitutions*, VII. 2. D. [622].

[60] Peter-Hans Kolvenbach, 'Le compte de conscience' (21 February 2005), *AR*, 23/1 (2003), 558.

opening one's conscience to the Local Superior should also be noted: 'A Jesuit may always open his conscience to his Local Superior—and indeed the latter would be permitted to request this if need be'.[61]

44. We ask Jesuits to refer to the Local Superior all questions that lie within his competence and not take these questions directly to the Major Superior.

45. In our present circumstances, it is not infrequent that Jesuits find themselves serving in works of the Society under a director of the work who may or may not be a Jesuit. In either case, Jesuits owe directors of the work complete, loyal cooperation in what pertains to their office. Jesuits are to make every effort to contribute to maintaining the work's Jesuit identity.

46. The Congregation wishes to express its profound gratitude to formed Jesuits of advanced years who have given their lives to the service of the Church. We also wish to remind them that they are as closely identified with the Lord when they serve him with reduced energies or even in sickness and suffering as they were when they went about 'proclaiming the kingdom in towns and villages'.[62] Those whose primary task is to pray for the Church and the Society are truly on mission, and their contribution to the Society's well-being and its service of the Kingdom can never be overemphasized, for they provide an example of placing oneself entirely in the hands of God, which can only inspire and console their brothers.

Superiors

47. The General Congregation encourages Major Superiors to exercise their roles with confidence and joy, to assign

[61] Kolvenbach, 'Le compte de conscience', 558; 'Guidelines for Local Superiors', 16, *AR*, 22/3 (1998), 369.

[62] Exx, 91.

Jesuits to their mission with clarity, and to show interest and care for the Jesuits they send on mission.

48. When Major Superiors name non-Jesuit directors of works, they should not only take into account candidates' professional competence but also their understanding and commitment to our mission and way of proceeding.

49. In the spirit of subsidiarity, we recommend that Major Superiors respect the scope for decision making that appropriately belongs to the Local Superior.

50. The General Congregation wants to emphasize once more the importance of the role of the Local Superior. Local Superiors need to receive the formation and preparation necessary for their mission. In this regard, Major Superiors are responsible for offering regular and timely courses and programmes to prepare Local Superiors.

51. The Local Superior shares with the whole community responsibility for the care and formation of Jesuits who have not yet pronounced final vows. Local Superiors are asked to take special care to request the account of conscience twice a year, to provide for the renewal of vows, and to ensure a community atmosphere that encourages the Jesuit in formation to grow as a person and as a religious.

52. It is important that community life be governed by clear directives. Local Superiors should collaborate with their brothers in working out and putting into practice a daily order and guidelines for common life. These practices should be evaluated at the time of the Major Superior's annual visit or other appropriate times.[63]

[63] *NC*, 319, 324.

Conclusion

53. Along his pilgrim way from Loyola to Rome, Ignatius prayed unceasingly to Mary, Our Lady, asking her to obtain for him the grace to be received under the banner of her Son.[64] In her expression, 'Here am I, the servant of the Lord; let it be with me according to your word',[65] Mary shows us how to live in total availability and to place our whole lives at the service of her Son. In her instruction to the servants at Cana, 'do whatever he tells you',[66] Mary points out for us the basic orientation that should guide our lives. For this reason, the Society has always seen in Mary a model of obedience.

54. Through the intercession of Mary, the Mother of the Lord, of St Ignatius and of the great company of brothers who have lived their lives of obedience with a love so profound that it has even led some to martyrdom, the Society rededicates itself to the practice of obedience 'for the greater service of God and for the more universal good'.[67]

[64] Exx, 147.

[65] Luke 1:38.

[66] John 2:5.

[67] *Constitutions*, VII.2.1. [618], VII.2.D. [622].

DECREE 5: Governance at the Service of Universal Mission

Introduction

1. General Congregation 35 establishes three principles to guide our consideration of governance in the Society of Jesus based on the experiences of recent decades and our apostolic mission:

a. *Our governance structures and ways of proceeding should flow from a perspective of greater universality.* This is in keeping with the directions set by previous General Congregations1 and responds to the accelerated pace of globalisation, the transnational and multicultural dimensions of the challenges facing the Church, and our desires to work more collaboratively throughout this universal Society.

b. *Structures of governance should be streamlined, modernised, and made more flexible where possible.* The Society is organized in function of its mission. We will serve that apostolic mission more effectively by simplifying some structures and procedures of governance, using modern methods of communication and collaboration, and introducing increasingly flexible structures at various levels.

c. *Changing circumstances require a better articulation of Ignatian values and ways of proceeding in our contemporary life and work.* Such changes as apostolic collaboration with others, the separation between apostolic institutions and community, and the development of an inter- and supra-provincial level of some ministries demand certain clarifications about how to exercise governance so that it might continue as genuinely Ignatian.

[1] Cf. GC 31, decree 48, n. 8; GC 32, decree 4, n. 81; GC 33, decree 1, n. 46; GC 34, decree 21.

Following from these principles, we offer some concrete directions for the different levels and organs of our current structure of governance.

I. General Governance

General Congregation

2. The General Congregation directs and authorises the General to undertake, in anticipation of General Congregation 36, a comprehensive revision of the Formula of a General Congregation, and of the Formulae of the Congregation of Procurators and of the Province Congregation.

3. The revised FCG should be approved by GC 36 in its first sessions. After consulting with the Major Superiors and receiving the approval of the General Council by deliberative vote, Father General may approve revisions in the FCG that would take effect before GC 36, as well as any related changes in the Formulae of the Congregation of Procurators and of the Province Congregation.

4. The revision should, in accord with the principles enunciated in the introduction (cf. n.1), aim at better facilitating the effective, responsible and adaptable use of the rich diversity of human and material resources that are employed in the preparation and conduct of a General Congregation, for the service of the life and mission of the universal Society. The revision should also respect, among other things, the following:

a. The threefold character of the General Congregation as:

a.1. the body which elects the General and which has a major role in the choice of the members of the General Council;

a.2. the highest instance of giving expression to the self-understanding of the universal body of the Society at a given moment; and

a.3. the supreme legislative body of the Society.

b. Given the traditional conviction that a General Congregation is an exceptional occurrence in the governance of the Society, its work should be confined to 'matters of greater moment' (FCG, 1 §2).

c. The importance of the whole Society's being represented in the General Congregation, especially in the Congregation *ad electionem*. In this context, at least two other matters are to be respected:

c.1. the number of elected members being greater than that of the appointed and *ex officio* members combined (cf. GC 34, decree 23A, n. 1);

c.2. the presence of an adequate number of Brothers as Electors.

d. With regard to the duration of the General Congregation: the need to balance, on the one hand, a responsible use of limited resources, and, on the other, the creation of an atmosphere of Ignatian discernment in the proceedings.

e. The need for a more thorough preparation of the General Congregation, especially in the work leading to the formulation of the *relationes praeviae* and the report *De statu Societatis*, but without prejudice to the freedom of the General Congregation itself to determine the content of its deliberations. Such preparation may require the role of a Province Congregation in preparing for a General Congregation to be expanded.

f. The rapid development of means of communication, as they affect both the preparation and the conduct of Congregations.

5. Of particular importance in preparing the General Congregation are the meetings of Major Superiors (cf. GC 34, decree 23 C, n.4), of Presidents of Conferences (cf. GC 34, decree 21, n.25) and of Electors of each Assistancy or Conference, and assemblies of various apostolic sectors. Each of these bodies could make a substantial contribution in the preparation of the General Congregation.

6. The Congregation of Procurators should be maintained, as representing the 'rank and file' of the membership of the Society. As indicated above, however, its Formula should be reviewed along with and in consequence of the revision of the FCG.

Central Governance

Principle

7. The Superior General is a source of unity in the universal body of the Society.[2] The Congregation recognises the rich diversity in the Society's membership and the inculturation necessary and proper for carrying out our mission within the universal Church and in an increasingly globalised world. As governance in the Society is always measured in an appropriate balance of union and diversity, the office of General must be exercised in a manner which respects diversity while placing it at the service of our universal mission and identity.

Reorganization

8. The General Congregation confirms the procedures to elect the four Assistants *ad providentiam* and to renew Father General's Council determined by GC 34, decree 23 E, II, n.1.

[2] *Constitutions*, VIII.1.6. [666], IX.1. [719].

9. In order that the General may have the most effective support for carrying out his responsibilities, he is directed by this General Congregation to undertake a comprehensive review of the central governance of the Society, with a view to reorganization for the service of mission.

10. Included in the purpose of this review is the provision of the resources and staff needed to handle the ordinary business of the Society, while allowing the General the opportunity to do comprehensive apostolic planning and to animate the whole body of the Society.

11. This review should take account of, but is not limited to:

a. the framework provided by *NC*, 380–386;

b. the need for communication among the various persons and groups mentioned in *NC*, 380–386, as well as between these persons and the General;

c. the need for coordination and articulation of the functions of these persons and groups;

d. the importance of avoiding unnecessary 'bureaucratisation' or unnecessary multiplication of officials and secretariats;

e. the importance of developing appropriate job profiles, which would involve regular articulation of goals and expected outcomes, together with an effective mechanism for review and evaluation.

12. The General is encouraged to look to ways in which finances might be used more effectively and equitably for the service of the international mission of the Society.

13. A professional and comprehensive strategy needs to be developed to improve our internal and external communications, so as to facilitate governance, foster

cooperation, and enhance the effectiveness of our universal mission.

14. The General is encouraged, in undertaking this review of central governance, to make use of the best professional assistance that is available within and outside the Society.

Evaluation

15. The General is asked to develop instruments and programmes for assisting all those in governance (central, conference, provincial and local) to review the effective implementation of and accountability for their proper responsibilities. *Practica quaedam* is to be updated to reflect these developments.

16. A review of the progress made in these matters should be included in the agenda of subsequent meetings with Presidents of Conferences. A more comprehensive report should be made at the next meeting with Major Superiors.

Conference of Major Superiors

Principles

17. Since we are aware that 'today many problems are global in nature and therefore require global solutions',[3] we consider the Conferences of Major Superiors—at present Africa and Madagascar, East Asia and Oceania, Europe, Latin America, South Asia and USA—to be a significant initiative in the governance structure of the Society.[4] While recognising the authority of the General for universal mission, we hold the conviction that today

[3] *NC*, 395 §1. Cf. also *NC*, 395–400.

[4] Cf. GC 34, decree 21, nn. 21–28.

cooperation among Provinces and Regions to realise the apostolic mission of the Society is an undeniable necessity.

18. The Conferences are expected to continue to be structural means that foster in all Jesuits a sense of universal mission, while facilitating union, communication, a common vision among the Superiors and inter- and supra-provincial cooperation. In order that the Conferences may respond more adequately to these aims, the following principles should be observed:

a. Conferences are structures orientated for mission and not mere instruments of inter-provincial coordination. They must continue doing apostolic planning at the inter-provincial level, taking into account the apostolic preferences of the universal Society. This apostolic planning is the result of discernment among the Major Superiors of the Conference, should be approved by the General, and should be evaluated and revised periodically.

b. Conferences are structures of cooperation among Provinces and Regions regarding specific inter- and supra-provincial aspects of mission (common works, formation centres, networking, inter-provincial teams, geographical regions, etc.). While Conferences do not constitute a new level of government between the General and the Provincials, they offer an opportunity to enhance the governance of Provincials by enabling them to care for the mission of the Society beyond their own Provinces.

c. Conferences have followed varying courses of development in the Society due to regional differences. The statutes of each Conference should, therefore, respect those differences and take into account the following:

c.1. The statutes are to be approved by the General and should include the following points: the membership, their rights and duties, the matters that come under the Conference's competence, the method of making decisions, internal structures, the authority and duties of the President (in accordance with nn. 19–23), and in general, whatever is considered necessary for an expeditious and efficient functioning of the Conference.

c.2. Each Conference should adapt its statutes in accordance with the orientations of GC 35.

d. Conferences should have the resources necessary to attend to the financial needs of works and houses dependent on the Conference.

President of the Conference

19. The General appoints the President after appropriate consultation with the Major Superiors of the Conference. He has the faculties of a Major Superior to carry out the specific responsibilities entrusted to him by the Statutes of the Conference.

20. The principles of unity of governance (*cura personalis, cura apostolica*), subsidiarity and sufficient authority to exercise one's office are to be applied appropriately to the role of Presidents of Conferences in this way:

a. Assignments:

a.1. In the area of his competence as defined in the Statutes, the President has authority to request and to assign persons from the Provinces or Regions needed for the activities and works dependent on the Conference. A basic criterion to make these assignments is that, all other things being equal, the needs of conference activities and works have priority over those of individual Provinces.[5]

[5] The second sentence of GC 34, decree 21, n. 24 is thus modified.

a.2. Respecting the centrality of the account of conscience in missioning, any such assignment requires the consultation of the man's Major Superior, who is the one who makes him available for a mission in the Conference.

a.3. In those rare situations in which the President and the respective Major Superior cannot come to an agreement regarding an assignment, the matter should be referred to the General for resolution.

b. Decision-making:

b.1. In the area of his competence as defined in the Statutes, the President is to make decisions as he sees fit, after having heard and considered attentively the views of the members of the Conference.

b.2. Although the President is endowed with the proper faculties to make decisions, it is necessary to emphasize the importance of his moral authority with the Provincials, which will enable him to propose objectives for collaboration and to promote discerned consensus among the Provincials. He himself needs to be an especially good leader, prudent, tactful and considerate.[6]

c. Relations with Provincials and Regional Superiors:

c.1. The existence of Conferences with their Presidents, as well as their decision-making authority in the inter- and supra-provincial sphere, implies that Provincials and Regional Superiors are involved in a new way of interconnection and interdependence, and are orientated towards cooperation.

c.2. The President does not have any direct authority in the internal governance of the Provinces nor does he supervise it. Provincials depend directly on the General. They are accountable to him in what concerns the

[6] *Constitutions*, VIII.1.G. [667].

internal governance of Provinces; they are accountable to the President in the strict area of his competence.

c.3. In exercising apostolic leadership, the President should be involved, as appropriate, in the apostolic discernment of Provinces and Regions.

21. The President is also the Major Superior of the common houses and works of the Conference, which the General has designated as such. In this sense,

a. The President, together with the other Major Superiors, has the responsibility to provide the human and financial resources needed for houses and works dependent on the Conference.

b. The President hears the manifestation of conscience of the Jesuits assigned on a stable basis to common houses and works.

c. The President has the responsibility for the ongoing formation and health care of the Jesuits assigned to common houses and works.

22. The President of the Conference attends a General Congregation as an *ex-officio* Elector.

23. The Presidents of Conferences shall meet together with the General at least once a year, or whenever called by him for consultation on important matters[7].

II. Province Governance

The Nature of the Province

24. While our vocation is to the universal Society, Provinces have been established for greater apostolic effectiveness and more effective governance so that the

[7] Cf. GC 34, decree 21, n. 25.

specific articulation of a Jesuit's mission is the direct result of the animating leadership of the Provincial.

Essential in this governance is the manifestation of conscience, conducted in an atmosphere of transparency and trust that enables the Provincial to assign men to specific ministries after discerning carefully how the holy desires, needs and gifts of his men meet the needs of the Province's apostolic plan and works alongside those of the Conference as well as the apostolic preferences established by the General.

25. Through the centuries, the structure of province governance has had much to commend it in apostolic and administrative efficiency: respect for varied cultural, linguistic, national and regional traditions, and the effective uniting of *cura personalis* with *cura apostolica.* Given today's globalised context within which Jesuits exercise ministry—sophisticated communications technologies, growing apostolic networks, and transnational realities—new challenges and new opportunities for ministry require reflection, formation, and concerted action that enables us to think and act across province and even conference boundaries.

This constantly evolving context calls for greater and better coordination and cooperation among Provinces (for example, in apostolic planning and financial administration) at the service of our universal mission. It also suggests a need for consideration of how Provinces can best be governed including the regular evaluation and review of effective governance, apostolic plans, administration of apostolic resources, and engagement with other Provinces through conference structures (cf. above, nn. 19–20).

26. With a view towards better serving our universal mission, the General Congregation requests the General to commission a process of reflection on Provinces and province structures which will lead to practical proposals

for adapting this aspect of our governance to today's realities. This commission's responsibility should include a comprehensive review of the criteria for the establishment (cf. *NC*, 388), reconfiguration, and suppression of Provinces and Regions. The criteria would include numerical and geographic size, age distribution, availability of effective leadership for governance and formation, financial viability, and capacity for developing a comprehensive apostolic plan which meets local, regional, and universal needs. The progress of this commission's work should be presented at the next meeting of Major Superiors.

Province and Local Church

27. It is particularly important that the Provincial actively pursue good communication and harmonious relationships with the Bishops of the local Churches in which we serve. This would include the expectation that local Superiors and directors of works be encouraged to do their part in the fostering of such relationships.

Province Planning and Decision-making

28. The Society's law (cf. especially *NC*, 354 §1) strongly encourages a participatory and discerning approach to decision-making at all levels, including that of the Province.[8] So that this approach may be even more effective, care needs to be taken that:

a. It remains clear that it is the appropriate Superior, not a consultative body, who makes the final decision (cf. *NC*, 354 §1).

b. There be sufficient clarity about the process for planning and decision-making, with the specific roles

[8] Cf. 'Guidelines for Provincials', 30–35, *AR*, 23/1 (2003), 297–298.

of various commissions and officials being adequately communicated to members of the Province.

c. The role of the Province Consultors, as laid down in universal and proper law,[9] be respected. This role should not be eroded by the responsibilities rightly given to staff, officials or commissions.

d. The Commission on Ministries (cf. *NC*, 260 §1) be an effective instrument for apostolic planning and its review, especially as this relates to established works and ministries of the Province, the creation of new apostolic works, and the ongoing apostolic formation of collaborators.

e. The legal and economic aspects of any decision should be considered.

f. There be structures for implementation and ongoing evaluation of the effectiveness of province plans.

Apostolic Works of the Province

29. Another critical aspect of the Provincial's governance is comprehensive care for the Province's apostolic works, including a thorough evaluation of their contribution to the Society's mission and of their Jesuit character. These works should be visited regularly by the Provincial (or his delegate; cf. *NC*, 391 §3), a report of which visit is to be included in his letters to the General. When the director of a work is someone other than a Jesuit, that director is expected to report on the work during the Provincial's visitation. A comprehensive articulation of the relationship between apostolic works (including international works of the Society) and the Province is expected and would include written agreements as helpful or required.

9 Cf. 'Guidelines for Provincials', 30, *AR*, 23/1 (2003), 297.

Training for Leadership

30. Leadership in the Society today is a very demanding ministry. The need for international cooperation, new structures for partnership with others, and heightened expectations about the quality of community life are only some of the factors that call for new attitudes and new skills in Superiors and directors of works at all levels of governance. Specific formation for Jesuits and others in positions of leadership is needed.

31. Ongoing formation in such attitudes and skills will often take place at the Province level, although there will also be many occasions when Conference-wide programmes will be extremely helpful. Critical areas for such training include:

a. principles of Ignatian leadership, including the practice of apostolic discernment in common;

b. formation in an attitude that enables one to work as a member of a team;[10]

c. principles of leadership in general;

d. management skills in areas such as: financial administration human resources planning conflict resolution confrontation conducting meetings crisis management media and public relations;

e. skills required for effective membership of a board of governance.

32. In addition to leadership training courses or workshops, there is great value in using forms of apprenticeship and mentoring. In appropriate ways potential leaders can

[10] Cf. 'Guidelines for the Relationship between the Superior and the Director of the Work', 16, *AR*, 22/3 (1998), 386–387.

be identified and be put in situations where they can learn from an experienced and wise leader.

III. Local Governance

Local Superior

Principles

33. The effectiveness of the Local Superior is critical to the apostolic vitality of the Jesuit community as a sign to the world of the Reign of God which we proclaim by our lives together. For Ignatius, love for the members of his community was to be the distinguishing mark of the Jesuit Superior.[11] From that starting point, the Superior can encourage the mission of apostolic men and ensure the quality of religious and community life that enables them to fulfil their mission.[12]

In a spirit of service, the Superior supports the members in their apostolic responsibilities and religious lives as servants of Christ's mission. These duties require an intimate knowledge of each man made possible by regular spiritual conversation and, where appropriate, manifestation of conscience. With such aids, the Superior can help each Jesuit to see how his apostolic work, assigned by the Major Superior, is properly integrated into the universal mission of the Society, promoting the sense of apostolic solidarity of all the community members, even of those who may be engaged in very diversified activities.[13]

34. From his privileged place at the heart of the community, the Superior is also responsible, together with each member, for developing its apostolic life.

[11] Cf. 'Guidelines for Local Superiors', 11, *AR*, 22/3 (1998), 368.

[12] Cf. 'Guidelines for Local Superiors', 33, *AR*, 22/3 (1998), 373.

[13] Cf. *NC*, 403 §2.

Concretely, this commits the Local Superior to leading his community in a Jesuit common life characterized by the celebration of Eucharist, prayer, faith sharing, communal discernment, simplicity, hospitality, solidarity with the poor, and the witness that 'friends in the Lord' can make to the world.

The General Congregation insists once again on the importance of the mission of local Superior and emphasizes the relevance of the points described in the *Complementary Norms*.[14]

Challenges

35. Actual practice has not always followed the guidelines presented in the *Complementary Norms*. The General Congregation recognises that several factors jeopardise the proper fulfilment of the mission entrusted to the Local Superior:

a. Communities are of different types: in some of them, Jesuits have received very different missions in a great variety of places; other communities are closely linked with the life of a particular apostolic work (directed by a member of the community or by another); other communities mix a number of Jesuits involved in the one apostolic work and other Jesuits whose missions take place in other institutions.

b. It is fundamental that every Jesuit be able to maintain a direct relationship with his Major Superior; but ready access to modern communication technologies can facilitate bypassing the Local Superior to communicate directly with the Major Superior in ways which undermine the proper relationship with the Local Superior.

[14] Cf. *NC*, 148, 151, 226, 323, 324, 349–354, 403, 406–407.

c. It is often too easy to minimise the importance of decision-making at the local level by concentrating too much authority at the provincial level, in apparent violation of the principle of subsidiarity in governance.

d. In some circumstances, relationships between Local Superiors and the director of the work, whether Jesuit or not, are a source of confusion and even conflict.

Recommendations

36. The General Congregation recommends that, in each Province or Conference of Major Superiors, formation sessions be developed in order to assist new Superiors to come to an understanding of their mission and to learn practical ways of carrying out that mission.

37. The General Congregation recommends that Major Superiors set up regular meetings of Local Superiors, with the following objectives: to promote mutual support among Superiors; to encourage discernment among those in charge of apostolates; and to facilitate ongoing formation in the mission of Local Superior.

38. The General Congregation recommends that Major Superiors allow for proper application of *NC* 351 by assuring that the Superior's primary responsibility is the animation of the local community.

39. The General Congregation recommends that Superiors acquire a good knowledge of the 'Guidelines for Local Superiors'. They are to make a responsible application of the Guidelines (i.e. adapted to the local situation), with particular attention given to the proper use of the house consult.[15]

[15] 'Guidelines for Local Superiors', 18, *AR*, 22/3 (1998) 369–370.

Superiors and Directors of the Work

40. The relations between Superiors and directors of the work must be developed in accordance with the 'Guidelines for the Relationship between the Superior and the Director of the Work'; these must be adapted to the local context in dialogue with the Major Superior.

41. The Superior must have a clear awareness of his responsibility regarding apostolic works and be prepared to exercise it. The director of a work must know to which Superior or provincial delegate he is called to give an account of his apostolic action.

42. It is important for the Major Superior to consider ahead of time the ways in which the relationship between the director and the relevant Local Superior will develop.[16] Often this relationship will also be formed with those in charge of institutions which are under the jurisdiction of civil law. Account must be taken of the requirements of both civil and canon law, and the relations between the two.

[16] Cf. 'Guidelines for the Relationship between the Superior and the Director of the Work', 18, 19, 23, 26–29, *AR*, 22/3 (1998), 387–388; *NC*, 406 § 1–2.

DECREE 6: Collaboration at the Heart of Mission[1]

Encouraging the Dynamism Initiated by GC 34

1. When Jesus wanted to teach his disciples about the power of the word of God, which every Jesuit ministry proclaims, he began: 'Listen! A sower went out to sow'.[2] He explained how some seed falls upon rocky ground, some among weeds, and other upon fertile soil where it yields a rich harvest. In his allocution to the members of GC 35, Pope Benedict XVI stressed the importance of the mission in which we are all engaged: 'make the Lord's true Face known to the many for whom he is still concealed or unrecognisable'.[3] He told us that the Church needs the Society, counts on it 'to reach the physical and spiritual places where others do not reach or have difficulty in reaching'.[4]

2. As men sent by the Vicar of Christ, we are led more and more to offer our gifts and to share with others the good news of the Kingdom. Following the inspiration of the Second Vatican Council, the Society of Jesus has been transformed by a profound movement of the Spirit. Recognising this, GC 34 approved the decree, 'Cooperation with the Laity in Mission', which both affirmed and encouraged apostolic collaboration, calling on Jesuits to cooperate with others in their projects and in ours.[5] GC 35, reviewing our own life and service to the Church, and

[1] 'Collaboration in mission' is described in different ways in various languages across the Society: Ignatian apostolic partners, partnership in mission, companions, collaborators, co-workers, colleagues. The common aspiration is apostolic companionship based on discernment and oriented towards service. In this document, we have simply used the word 'collaboration'.

[2] Mark 4:3.

[3] Benedict XVI, allocution, § 4.

[4] Benedict XVI, allocution, § 2.

[5] GC 34, decree 13, n. 7.

noting how the seeds which have been scattered through the inspiration of GC 34 are yielding a harvest 'thirty and sixty and a hundredfold',[6] renews our commitment to apostolic collaboration and to a profound sharing of labour for the life of the Church and the transformation of the world.

3. We are humbled and grateful that so many—inspired as we have been by the vocation of Ignatius and the tradition of the Society—have chosen both to work with us and to share our sense of mission and our passion to reach out to the men and women of our broken but lovable world. We are enriched by members of our own faith, but also by people from other religious traditions, those women and men of good will from all nations and cultures, with whom we labour in seeking a more just world. Rich is the harvest. In many countries, important Jesuit works depend largely on the generous, loyal and skilled collaboration of women and men of diverse religious and humanistic convictions. As the Holy Father affirmed our ministry and mission, saying to us, 'The Church needs you', we must in turn look to our collaborators in mission and say, with gratitude and affection, that the call we have received is a call shared by us together.

Challenges and Responses since GC 34

4. Since GC 34 we have learned much. In some regions the development of collaboration has been limited because the participation of lay people in the local Church is minimal. In other regions, where Christians are in the minority, the challenge rests on bringing an awareness of the Ignatian charism to those whose spiritual experiences are often far different. Furthermore, in places oppressed by mass

[6] Mark 4: 8.

culture, the distractions of exaggerated individualism and consumerism have encouraged resistance to the powerful call of community and service found in our mission. Furthermore, our own uncertainty, born of the changing face of our ministries in a time of growing collaboration, has led to some hesitation and even resistance to a full engagement with the call of GC 34.

5. At the same time, the powerful spirit acknowledged and encouraged by GC 34 has not been idle, and for every challenge greater creativity and zeal have been the response. Numerous programmes of Ignatian formation have grown up around the world, adapted to various religious and cultural contexts. The foundational grace of the Spiritual Exercises is more widely available and provides a common language and experience, in which collaboration in mission is rooted and inspired. Increasing numbers of Jesuit works are directed by committed lay people, by other religious, and by diocesan clergy. The members of the Society—priests and brothers, those formed and those in formation—have a greater awareness of shared responsibility with others for the mission and ministry of the Society. Further, the Society has been enriched by our encounter with diverse communities of dialogue and cooperation. Lay and religious, women and men, indigenous persons and those of different religious and spiritual experiences: all these have changed us and nurtured in us a greater sense of the God in whom 'we live and move and have our being'.[7] The grace of these years is reflected in both more extensive and deeper apostolic collaboration, which places all—Jesuits and others—with the Son.

6. The seeds of mission sown by our collaboration have actually yielded a rich harvest, for the Ignatian charism

[7] Acts 17:28.

serves not just the Society but the whole Church. We are aware of the contribution of this Ignatian charism in forming an apostolic laity, a development called for by the Vatican Council and identified by GC 34 as 'a grace of our day and a hope for the future'.[8]

Orientations for Furthering Collaboration

7. While GC 34 recognised the Spirit's movement and opened for us fresh avenues to implement our mission through more profound collaboration with the laity, the current Congregation recognises the more diverse community of those with whom we have been called to share this common mission. The seeds sown by grace are growing in many ways and in many lands, and we wish to support this growth, while also indicating some other ways by which that growth might be fostered.

8. In this decree we wish especially to reflect upon the way in which collaboration in mission calls us to a new and often challenging renewal of our ministries. This renewal demands that we address the following questions: what constitutes a Jesuit work, and how might it be sustained with other than Jesuits in leadership? What are the necessary elements of formation needed by Jesuits and others to ensure growth in the spirit and practice of our mission? What bonds might appropriately unite us as collaborators in mission who seek to serve together, with deepening affection, the mission given to the Society?

What Constitutes and Sustains a Jesuit Work?

9. The heart of an Ignatian work is the Spiritual Exercises of Ignatius. Indeed, any work may be said to be *Ignatian* when it manifests the Ignatian charism: i.e., when it intentionally *seeks God in all things*; when it practises

[8] Vatican II, *Apostolicam actuositatem*, 29; GC 34, decree 13, n. 1.

Ignatian discernment; when it engages the world through a careful analysis of context, in dialogue with experience, evaluated through reflection, for the sake of action, and with openness, always, to evaluation. Such a work does not rely necessarily upon the Society of Jesus for its Ignatian identity, though it may affiliate with the Society in partnership through networks and other structures.

10. An *Ignatian* work can be said to be *Jesuit* when it has a clear and definitive relationship with the Society of Jesus and when its mission accords with that of the Society by a commitment to a faith that does justice through interreligious dialogue and a creative engagement with culture. In such a context, the mission of the work, whether administered by a Jesuit or by another who shares this commitment, will be 'ultimately accountable to the General of [the] Society through appropriate lines of authority'.[9]

11. The leadership of a Jesuit work depends upon commitment for mission and can be exercised by Jesuits or by others. Such leaders must have a commitment to the mission of the Society as realised in the particular work, though they may be of religious or spiritual traditions different from our own. Clarity about the mission of each apostolic work and the respective roles of all parties prevents misunderstandings, promotes greater accountability and builds teamwork. All those in leadership should understand and affirm these varied responsibilities in order to be better able to participate in the discernment and decision-making processes regarding matters of mission.

12. In developing a relationship between the Society and a Jesuit work, it is vital that Major Superiors engage

[9] 'Guidelines for the Relationship between the Superior and the Director of the Work', 9, *AR*, 22/3 (1998) 385; 'Instruction on the Administration of Goods', 109–111.

and support those entrusted with leadership, whether Jesuit or other. Regular dialogue, conducted in a spirit of trust and with respect for appropriate subsidiarity, serves to promote discernment, accountability and a clearer sense of collaboration for mission. Further, the Provincial or others should provide such leaders with important information and directives from the wider Society of Jesus, thus encouraging a broader vision of mission and a better understanding of apostolic priorities and criteria.

13. The local Jesuit Superior and local Jesuits do much to foster the connection between a Jesuit ministry and the Society. All Jesuits, but especially those assigned to a work, can help to foster a spirit of discernment and collaboration by their example and their willingness to share their lives with others. Likewise, our communities, as apostolic centres and not as mere residences, are called to explore how their hospitality may promote collaboration.

14. Recommendations:

> a. We encourage Father General to revise the 'Guidelines for the Relationship between the Superior and the Director of the Work' to provide effective support for all those in positions of responsibility, whether Jesuits or others, and to assist all parties in the understanding of their various roles and responsibilities. This document should recognise the multiplicity of contexts and give parameters that foster unity while allowing appropriate diversity.
>
> b. We encourage Major Superiors (and Conferences, where appropriate) to develop provincial or regional guidelines for endorsing and sponsoring Jesuit works.
>
> c. We encourage Major Superiors (and Conferences, where appropriate) to develop tools to evaluate the effectiveness of Jesuit ministries in accomplishing their mission.

d. We encourage local Jesuit communities to explore ways of offering hospitality and support for the development of collaboration in mission.

What are the Elements of Formation for Collaborative Mission?

15. Collaboration in mission has resulted in abundant blessings for the apostolates and the Society of Jesus. Being with apostolic collaborators in mission encourages us to live more fully and authentically our Jesuit religious vocation. Ultimately, we bring to these relationships our own identity as men of the vows and of the *Constitutions*, men whose experience of the Spiritual Exercises has bound us to one another and to a particular 'pathway to God'.[10] In collaboration with others, in respectful dialogue and shared reflection, in labour alongside those similarly engaged who walk a different pathway, we come to know our own journey better and to follow it with new zeal and understanding.

16. From the earliest stages of Jesuit formation and throughout our lives as Jesuits, training in collaboration must be experiential, not only informing our understanding of ministry but moulding our identity as men for others who are also men with others.[11] The vital role of collaboration for our way of proceeding as Jesuit ministers has implications for the content and methodology of formation as well as for the role of *formatores*.

17. Likewise, the importance of collaboration in mission means that all Jesuits, as men on mission, must also be men of collaboration. Ongoing formation in this area should be encouraged and supported within Provinces and

[10] Formula of the Institute, *Constitutions*, 1.

[11] GC 34, decree 13, n. 4.

throughout Jesuit Conferences. When undertaken together with collaborators, programmes of professional development and spiritual enrichment can help us deepen our sense of common vision and our unity in mission.

18. The formation of Jesuits for collaboration, however, must be accompanied by a parallel formation of those with whom we minister, so that they might deepen their understanding of the mission they share with us. Diverse programmes that respect and draw upon the wisdom and experience of the participants allow for a personal appropriation of the mission of the Society. Respecting various levels of connection and understanding, these programmes invite each person—whether employee or volunteer, newly arrived or veteran, Christian believer, member of another faith community or person without a religious affiliation—into a deeper awareness of his or her place in the Ignatian and Jesuit mission.

19. Such formation should provide professional skills, develop a special understanding of Ignatian spirituality regarding mission, and include opportunities for growth in the interior life. Part VII of the *Constitutions*, the *Complementary Norms*, and the *Autobiography* of St Ignatius provide important insights, although the *Spiritual Exercises* is always primary.

20. A final dimension of formation for mission involves programmes of preparation and support for collaborators in leadership positions. All those in leadership positions have a special relationship with the Society of Jesus. Since their challenging work is important for the mission of the Society, they need ongoing support and care from the Society and one another. Furthermore, they should receive suitable formation in the distinctive dimensions of our way of proceeding, especially the integration of apostolic discernment in decision-making.

21. Recommendations:

a. We encourage Conferences and Assistancies to examine the programme of Jesuit formation to ensure that all men in formation have appropriate experience of collaborative ministry.

b. We encourage Major Superiors (and Conferences, where appropriate) to assist in the continuing development of opportunities and structures for the ongoing formation of Jesuits in collaborative ministry.

c. We encourage Major Superiors (and Conferences, where appropriate) to assist in the continuing development of opportunities and structures for the formation of others who collaborate in the mission of the Society.

d. We encourage Major Superiors (and Conferences, where appropriate) to ensure the development of opportunities and structures for the appropriate formation of those in leadership positions in Jesuit ministries.

What Connections Might Make Our Work More Fruitful?

22. As means of communication develop, the Society works more effectively as an international body and seeks synergies in service of its universal mission. Jesuits are often engaged beyond their province boundaries in national and international networks and in collaboration with a variety of persons, including other Jesuits. Some of these international networks such as the Jesuit Refugee Service, Fe y Alegría, and the African Jesuit AIDS Network are works of the Society. Others are collaborative projects. In all such works, however, the good accomplished is multiplied by participation of the Society in collaboration with diverse parties united in a common mission.

23. GC 34 invited the Society to develop an 'Ignatian Apostolic Network'[12] among persons and associations that share an Ignatian commitment to service in the Church. In those places in which the Society has responded zealously to this call, cooperation is growing in programmes for formation as well as in the discernment, planning and execution of common projects. These networks enable men and women with common concerns to share their experience and make use of their expertise. In this they realise the ever-widening possibilities of our networking. Moreover, the Ignatian tradition, when expressed by various voices—women and men, religious and lay, movements and institutions, communities and individuals—becomes more welcoming and more vigorous, capable of enriching the whole Church.

24. The Society desires strong relationships in mission with as many collaborators in the Lord's vineyard as possible. Those asking to be more closely linked with the mission of the Society[13] normally come to this desire through an experience of the Spiritual Exercises.

25. Among the many different forms of collaboration, GC 34 considered a specific 'closer personal bond' between individuals and the Society, whereby a lay person could be missioned by a Provincial. This relationship implies mutual commitments by the Society and the individual.[14] Sometimes called a 'juridical bond', this manner of collaboration was authorised and recommended by GC 34 for an experimental period of ten years, subject to evaluation by GC 35.

[12] GC 34, decree 13, n. 21.

[13] Cf. Peter-Hans Kolvenbach, 'Concernant les laics associés' (25 February 2003), *AR*, 23/1 (2003), 102–103. In English as 'On Lay Associates', letter to all Major Superiors, 2003/08.

[14] GC 34, decree 13, nn. 23–25.

26. GC 35 affirms that this experiment was meant to be spiritual and mission-focused,[15] rather than legal or canonical. Over the last thirteen years, the experience of this specific form of 'closer personal bond' has not been widespread in the Society, nor was there much demand for it. Some individuals became devoted to our common mission in this way, and they have contributed much to it. Occasionally, however, misperceptions arose as to what mutual expectations were, and collaborators without such a relationship wondered whether their manner of collaboration was somehow less valued than those with the 'closer personal bond'.

27. GC 35 acknowledges with sincere gratitude the contribution that has been made to the Society of Jesus and its mission by these experiences. However, after reviewing them, the Congregation concludes that it is preferable no longer to promote the special kind of spiritual bond which GC 34 described in decree 13, nn.23–25. Those who have already entered into this closer personal bond with the Society should be able to continue in it as long as Local Provincials discern with them that it is the best way to proceed in mission. But this option for such a specific 'closer personal bond' should no longer be open to new candidates. As we continue to accompany those desiring to work in the mission of the Society, we can encourage them to live their vocation in one of the many ways of collaboration with which the Church has been blessed, especially since Vatican II has so clearly spelled out the mission of the laity in the Church.

[15] This bond between the Society and the individual 'is by its nature spiritual and apostolic, not legal'. Peter-Hans Kolvenbach, 'Sobre la "vinculación jurídica" de los laicos a la Compañía' (17 March 1999), *AR*, 22/4 (1999), 530–533. In English as 'On "Juridical Bonding" between Lay People and the Society', letter to all Major Superiors, 1999/04.

Among these are an increasing number of associations inspired by Ignatian spirituality.

28. We note with gratitude and joy the many autonomous associations with whom we share a spiritual bond, the fruit of which is greater and more effective service to the mission of Christ in the world. Among these, the Christian Life Community has roots that are deep in the charism and history of the Society. We wish to continue to support CLC in its journey towards ever greater apostolic effectiveness and collaboration with the Society. Likewise, other Ignatian groups, including Jesuit alumni/ae associations, various Jesuit volunteer organizations, the Apostleship of Prayer, the Eucharistic Youth Movement, and many others deserve our continued spiritual accompaniment as well as our support for their apostolic service.

29. Recommendations:

a. We encourage the Society's government at all levels to explore means by which more effective networking might take place among all apostolic works associated with the Society of Jesus.

b. We encourage the Society's government at all levels to explore with other communities of Ignatian inspiration, both religious and lay, ways to promote and support an 'Ignatian Family' or 'Ignatian Community' which will have a common vision of service, will promote networks of mutual support, and will foster new and closer forms of collaboration locally, regionally and internationally.

c. We encourage Superiors, especially Major Superiors, to seek ways to support and accompany CLC and other Ignatian inspired autonomous associations locally, regionally, and nationally.

Conclusion

30. In his day, St Ignatius gave shelter to the homeless of Rome, cared for prostitutes, and established homes for orphans. He sought collaborators and with them established organizations and networks to continue these and many other forms of service. To respond today to the pressing needs of our complex and fragile world, many hands are surely needed. Collaboration in mission is the way we respond to this situation: it expresses our true identity as members of the Church, the complementarity of our diverse calls to holiness,[16] our mutual responsibility for the mission of Christ,[17] our desire to join people of good will in the service of the human family, and the coming of the Kingdom of God. It is a grace given to us in this moment, one consistent with our Jesuit way of proceeding.

[16] Cf. John Paul II, *Vita consecrata*, 12.

[17] 1 Corinthians 12:12 ff.

Mass of the Election, 19 January 2008

Other Documents of the General Congregation

1. Issues for the Ordinary Government of the Society of Jesus Studied at the 35th General Congregation[1]

Once the election of Father General was concluded, the 35th General Congregation began to deal with agenda, *negotia*. To do this they accepted the proposal of the *coetus praevius* to organize the postulates by topics and to consider two main categories. One category consisted of five topics which were proposed for decrees: mission, identity, government, obedience and laity; the other category consisted of five topics which were proposed as possible recommendations or mandates for the ordinary government of the Society: community, formation, vocation promotion, youth ministry and the Jesuit Refugee Service.

After gathering the suggestions which had been made by the Electors in meetings according to Assistancy, the General Congregation added ten other topics which were judged appropriate for consideration. With these additions the list of topics proposed for ordinary government was the following:

[1] The General Congregation decided that, together with the official decrees of the Congregation, a narrative document should be published dealing with the discussions of the topics for the ordinary government, without including the suggestions directed to Father General. This document was entrusted to Father General, with the deliberative vote of the Fathers of the Curia who have the right to participate in a General Congregation due to their office.

Africa
Intellectual apostolate
International Houses in Rome
Communications
China
Ecology, environment and globalisation
Finances
Formation
Religious fundamentalism and dialogue
Brothers
Youth ministry
Migrants and refugees
Indigenous peoples
Community life
Vocations

The Congregation decided to form commissions to deal with these topics. Each commission prepared a document which was then presented and discussed in a plenary session. After receiving reactions, the commissions made proposals for action on the part of the ordinary government of the Society. In other plenary sessions the opinion of the General Congregation was sought by means of a vote. Some of the approved proposals were included in decrees; others were presented to Father General for his government; still others were directed to the Provinces and Conferences of Provincials and are included in this document.

The following is a summary of the discussions in the commissions and in the plenary sessions of the 35th General Congregation.

Africa: The delegates of the African Assistancy to the 35th General Congregation asked the Society to join their efforts to promote a better understanding of the continent. The negative image frequently presented by the media must be changed. We need to foster respect and unified action.

In Africa good work is being done in Jesuit institutions and there are advocacy efforts to prevent the forced displacement of peoples and the exploitation of resources. These initiatives, however, are not well known.

The African Jesuits are grateful for the international collaboration which has been offered to them and they invite Jesuits throughout the world to continue to join their apostolic efforts. Even though their continent has many needs, they offer themselves to collaborate in the universal mission of the Society beyond their own borders.[1]

Intellectual apostolate: As the commission assigned to study this topic reflected on the tradition of the Society and the recent urging of Benedict XVI,[2] it originally proposed a decree. In the end it made three recommendations. First, young Jesuits should be encouraged to consider this apostolate and to be assigned to it. In spite of the cost and time involved, it is indispensable to promote special studies among them without neglecting care for their personal and community life. Secondly, it is crucial that the intellectual apostolate foster every possible form of collaboration among persons, teams, centres and journals, promote working in networks and choose institutions which can assure excellence in research. Thirdly, Conferences and Provincials should care for the conservation and preservation of our intellectual patrimony or its distribution.[3]

International Houses in Rome: After an introduction to the topic by Father General's delegate, the commission met with the members of the CIP (Permanent Inter-provincial Commission for the Roman Houses), which explained its programme. It is important to engage in planning which involves not only a general framework for these works but also a reorganization and integration of administrative structures, as well as an

[1] Africa is one of the global preferences established by GC 35, decree 3, n. 39 (i).

[2] Benedict XVI, 'To the Members of the Society of Jesus' (22 April 2006), *AR*, 23/4 (2006), 676–679; allocution,

[3] The intellectual apostolate is a global preferences established by the GC35, decree 3, n. 39 (iii).

improvement in the networking among them. There is need to design a relevant pedagogical plan which includes not only the formation of professors and administrative staff but also the recruitment of highly talented students. The commission pointed out some *ad intra* tasks: the relationships between Superiors and directors of the Roman institutions and between the delegate and the Provincials, the type of religious community which is helpful to young professors and the reentry of retiring professors into their Provinces.[4]

Communications: The commission appointed to discuss this topic first pointed out how important the world of communications is for our vocation as evangelizers. Our whole history bears witness to the efforts that have been made to find better and more effective means to evangelize. We are, however, in a new world. Modern means of communication and new technologies demand that we adapt our way of proceeding to today's generation which lives in a continuous process of change.[5] The commission also spoke about concrete topics, for example a review of the norms for publication and a possible broadening of them to include what is placed on the Internet. The General Congregation asked that communication be given special attention during formation and it urged Provinces and Conferences to promote creative and apostolic use of the Internet.

China: The 35th General Congregation discussed the situation of China because this country has become a global power which cannot be neglected. The commission charged with this topic explained how experts on China view its economic power, its impressive rate of growth, the rapid decrease in poverty and areas of tension. The commission spoke about

[4] The Roman Houses are a global preference established by GC 35, decree 3 n. 39 (iv).

[5] Cf. GC 35, decree 3, n. 29.

advances in the area of religious freedom as well as the positive contribution which persons of different faiths have made to the construction of a better Chinese society. Finally, the commission mentioned the letter of Benedict XVI to Catholics in China[6] and the generally positive reaction which it received.[7]

Ecology, environment and globalisation: The 35th General Congregation wished to discuss these topics as a whole and appointed a commission for this task. During the discussion which took place in a plenary session, reference was made to the magnitude and complexity of this phenomenon.[8] For this reason it is essential that we collaborate with individuals and institutions in establishing networks. In collaborating with others, Jesuits must not forget the specific contribution which the Christian faith can make to this topic. It is sad that the contribution of the Society[9] in this area is too little known and made use of, even by Jesuits. The General Congregation recommends that the Provinces draw up guidelines so that individual Jesuits as well as Jesuit communities and institutions may use their resources in an ecologically responsible way.

Finances: In a plenary session the General Treasurer of the Society presented the economic situation of the Society in the context of the world economic situation. He emphasized how this situation affects the resources available to many Provinces and the capacity of the Society to obtain and distribute them. He stressed the necessity of making decisions which would lead to a better use of the resources which are available. To achieve this goal Jesuits are needed who

6 Benedict XVI, letter to the bishops, presbyters [etc.] … of the Catholic Church in the People's Republic of China, 27 May 2007.

7 China is a global preference established by GC 35, decree 3, n. 39 (ii).

8 Cf. GC 35, decree 3, nn. 31–36.

9 Secretariat for Social Justice, *Promotio Iustitiae*, 70 (April 1999); *Globalisation and Marginalisation*.

are competent in planning, administration and accounting, and who can assure transparency and good management. The General Treasurer suggested some concrete courses of action: the creation of adequate structures to obtain funds, the reinforcement of mechanisms for reaching decisions with the help of advisers and consultants, a knowledge and application of the Statutes on Poverty and the Instruction on the Administration of Goods, and the formation of men in administration.

Formation: In a plenary session the commission in charge of this topic presented the positive and negative aspects of formation in the Society. Among the successes are the excellent documents for all stages of formation and greater inter-provincial collaboration. On the negative side, mention must be made of the difficulty in adapting formation to the diverse candidates who come to the novitiate, as well as of the rapid rate of cultural change which affects young men and hinders their integration into the Jesuit way of proceeding. It is a challenge for formation to find not only adequate pedagogies but also a sufficient number of trained men who are able to work in formation. There was a consensus that the main 'formator' is the body of the Society and that all Jesuits, therefore, must assume their part of the responsibility for formation.

Religious fundamentalism and dialogue: From the beginning this commission stressed the multifaceted character of fundamentalism. Jesuits have to make an effort to understand it in all its complexity. The 35th General Congregation reaffirmed the commitment of the Society to interreligious and cultural dialogue and recognised the work being carried out in this field.[10] Now Jesuits are asked to accept the difficult task of expanding this dialogue to religious fundamentalism,

[10] GC 35, decree 3, nn. 3–4.

of entering into contact with it, of improving activities in networks, and of cooperating with secretariats and organizations committed to dialogue.

Brothers: The commission appointed by the 35th General Congregation was composed mostly of Brothers and presented several practical proposals in a plenary session. The commission first proposed that the government of the Society always keep the Brothers in mind when planning programmes for studies for Jesuits in formation. It was suggested there be some programmes of formation specifically for Brothers, as is already being done in some parts of the Society. The 'Alphonsus Month' would be an example. Attention should be given to the ongoing formation of formed Brothers.

Youth ministry: Although only three postulates on this topic were received, the General Congregation decided to appoint a commission to study it. After reviewing the most successful experiences, the commission identified the principal points of youth ministry and the new challenges emerging since the 34th General Congregation. The reality of young people depends on the geographical context. In some areas what is needed is listening to young people and promoting a deeper spirituality; in other areas the accent is on inviting young people to participate in social projects or in reaching out to and engaging young people who are not involved. The Congregation suggests that each Conference consider whether it would be helpful to appoint a coordinator of youth ministry.

Migrants and refugees: In a presentation during a plenary session, the commission noted that, since the founding of the Jesuit Refugee Service in 1980, the phenomenon of 'people in movement' has become more complex. Some migrants move to another country of their own free will; others are forced to move, sometimes to another place within their own country, because of war, natural disasters or even human trafficking. They are received with hostility and weak legal structures do not protect their rights. The General Congregation asks that the Society continue to support the JRS with the assignment of Jesuits and other resources and to promote close collaboration between the Provinces and Conferences and the JRS. It also urges all Provinces, through their institutions, to promote the integration of migrants into the society which receives them.[11]

Indigenous peoples: The 35th General Congregation received numerous postulates on this topic. In a plenary session the commission which studied them emphasized the fact that today there about 370 million indigenous people[12] spread throughout the world and that they represent a rich cultural heritage and an important legacy of civilisation. Because of various political and socio-economic factors, the indigenous peoples are among the most marginalised and exploited. The process of globalisation, which is partly responsible for environmental degradation and the pillage of natural resources, has a particular effect on them. In addition, climate change continues seriously to harm them. Since this situation threatens the very survival of these peoples, the Society should increase its commitment to them. The General Congregation suggests that in every area where this challenge exists, the Conference of Provincials form 'work groups' of Jesuits working in this apostolate.

Community life: The commission which was charged with this topic originally wanted to make a decree. Although the proposal was not accepted, the plenary session provided the opportunity for a rich discussion on community as a part of the mission of the Society

[11] This is another global preference established in GC 35, decree 3, n. 39 (v).

[12] Cf. United Nations: Permanent Forum on Indigenous Issues (UNPFII), 1.

and not merely as a locus for its members to restore their energies for the apostolate. It was stated that the Kingdom of God has need of clear signs in this world and that the quality of our community life is one of them. This presupposes grace, but also an effort to experience personal and community conversion, to share faith, to discern and to adopt an austere lifestyle close to the poor. If Jesuit communities are not going to be mere residences but signs of the Kingdom of God, the office of Superior, according to the Ignatian way of proceeding, has to assume its crucial importance.

Vocations: The commission evaluated the implementation of Fr Kolvenbach's letter on vocation promotion. It paid particular attention to the cultural changes which make the countercultural and lifelong commitment of a religious very difficult. There has certainly been progress in this area. There is a growing awareness that all Jesuits are responsible for vocation promotion.[13] Stable structures have been set up for vocational promotion and follow-up. The Society has greater experience of and confidence in the pedagogy of the Exercises as applied to young men. Some problems still remain, such as the lack of articulation between youth and vocational ministry and the lack of spiritual directors for young men. Some Jesuits, unfortunately, are not convinced and concerned about vocation promotion.

The General Congregation invites the Society to put into practice what has already been established on these topics and hopes that the treatment that has been given here will be an effective aid in the ordinary government of the Society.

(original in Spanish)

[13] Peter-Hans Kolvenbach, 'Sobre la promoción de vocaciones' (29 September 1997), *AR*, 22 (1996–2002), 158–161.

Letter of the Members of GC 35 to Fr Kolvenbach

The Thirty-fifth General Congregation of the Society of Jesus

Tuesday 4 March 2008

The Reverend Father Peter-Hans Kolvenbach SJ
Curia Generalizia della Compagnia di Gesù
Borgo Santo Spirito 4
CP 1639 ROMA

Dear Father Kolvenbach,

The Peace of Christ!

On the morning of Saturday 1 March, shortly before you took your leave of us, we had the opportunity to thank you in person for the outstanding contribution you made to our Society during your 24 years and more as Superior General. Our farewell came from the heart: both the warm words of Fr Nicolás and our spontaneous and affectionate response expressed not only our sentiments but those of our brother Jesuits around the world.

We could not end this General Congregation, however, without providing you with this written record of our gratitude and esteem, one which gives brief and no doubt inadequate expression to our conviction that your years as General have been a great grace for us. For this grace, we now give God thanks as we shall no doubt continue to do for a long time to come.

Many of us have reason to know something of the burdens carried by those in leadership positions in the Church and of the increasing complexity of their work. As over the years we have set about our many tasks, we have been unfailingly supported by your own devotion to duty. This involved a daily schedule of work that would have taxed a man many years younger than yourself.

We have all benefited from your wisdom, your sense of humour, your precise attention to detail and your already legendary capacity to remember people and places in our Provinces, often better than we can ourselves. On a number of occasions during this Congregation we have had reason to appreciate once again the fruits of your profound sense of *sentire cum Ecclesia* and of your devotion to our vocation 'to serve as a soldier of God beneath the banner of the Cross ... and to serve the Lord alone and his Church, under the Roman Pontiff, the Vicar of Christ on Earth'.

Your governance was also always personal. Your many letters, your lunches with those visiting the Curia, and your visits to our Provinces and Regions, where you met so many Jesuits and collaborators, shook as many hands and participated in numerous meetings, made the central government of the Society present to us in a way that has both inspired us and encouraged us.

The challenges that faced the Society in the years of your generalate were considerable. These were years of rapid change both in the Church and in the wider world, changes from which the Society could not be, nor would wish to be, immune.

It was your gift to motivate us to take up the opportunities for mission provided by these new contexts. As our work expanded on the new geographical frontiers of the Church, we also explored those equally challenging frontiers where many faiths and cultures meet. While it was always your way to support Provincials in the exercise of their local responsibilities, you nonetheless challenged us to respond generously to the universal mission of the

Society and to put our sometimes scarce resources at the service of the greater need. The development of Conferences of Major Superiors, which you promoted, and the apostolic preferences for the whole Society, which you identified, will surely enable this more universal perspective to come to still greater prominence in the years ahead.

It was always your desire to encourage the Society in its life with the Lord and in its fidelity to the Ignatian charism. To this end, you wrote us many inspirational letters, on aspects of formation, discernment, poverty, community life and the Eucharist, to name but a few. These were all the more valuable to us because they were clearly informed by your own personal prayer and reflection.

In these letters, as in your articles, addresses, talks and homilies, you taught us to ground ourselves in the experience of the First Companions. At the same time, you demonstrated an acute understanding of the challenges which face those who live our life today. What you have written will nourish the quality of our religious life for many years to come. The attention you gave to bringing the *Complementary Norms* to fruition, moreover, will long remain a sign to us of the care we should have for the *Constitutions* of our Society.

Meanwhile, you also encouraged us to be not only 'men for others' but 'men with others'. You have seen, as we have, so much new energy and enthusiasm coming to our service of the Church from those many others who have also been called to follow the path of Ignatius and with whom we now more readily, and more constructively, collaborate in mission.

Nowhere has this collaboration borne more fruit than in our service of the poor, not least in our accompaniment of refugees and forced migrants. The work of the Jesuit Refugee Service has, with your unflagging support, expanded considerably during your years as General. It is just one of the many ways in which we give witness both to a faith that does justice and to our conviction that we cannot be companions of Jesus unless we are also companions, as he was, with those who have least.

During the Jubilee Year, which you opened in December 2005, you reminded us that our vocation is above all a missionary vocation, as it was for Francis Xavier, which has its origins in that ever deeper encounter with Jesus himself in the Spiritual Exercises of Ignatius. This vocation finds its expression in that warm and devoted companionship epitomized by Pierre Favre: a companionship with Jesus, with one another and with those whom it is our privilege to serve as we engage in our mission of faithful service to the Church. This was the vocation you promoted among us and you did so, first and foremost, by embodying it yourself.

May the Lord bless you with safe travels, good health and many years of happiness as you return to serve the Church and the Society in Lebanon.

While assuring you of our continued prayers, our very best wishes and our profound gratitude, we remain,

Your devoted brothers in Christ,

The Members of the Thirty-fifth General Congregation of the Society of Jesus

Benedict XVI and Fr Adolfo Nicolás

Complementary Documentation

Benedict XVI

1. Benedict XVI to Fr Kolvenbach, 10 January 2008

To the Reverend Father Peter-Hans Kolvenbach SJ
Superior General of the Society of Jesus

1. On the occasion of the 35th General Congregation of the Society of Jesus, I fervently wish to offer to you and all who are taking part in the Assembly my most cordial greeting, together with the assurance of my affection and my constant spiritual closeness. I know how important for the life of the Society the event being celebrated is and, furthermore, that it has consequently been prepared with great care. This is a providential opportunity to impress upon the Society of Jesus that renewed ascetic and apostolic thrust which is hoped for by all, so that the Jesuits may fully accomplish their mission and face the challenges of the modern world with that fidelity to Christ and to the Church which marked the prophetic action of St Ignatius of Loyola and his First Companions.

2. The Apostle wrote to the faithful of Thessalonica, recalling that he had proclaimed God's gospel to them: 'urging and encouraging you and pleading', he explained, 'that you lead a life worthy of God, who calls you into his own kingdom and glory',[1] and he added:

> We also constantly give thanks to God for this, that when you received the word of God that you heard from us, you accepted it not as a human word but as

[1] 1 Thessalonians 2:12.

> what it really is, God's word, which is also at work in you believers.[2]

God's Word, therefore, is first 'received', that is, listened to, and then, as it penetrates the heart, it is welcomed, and those who receive it recognise that God speaks through his messenger: in this way his Word acts in believers. As it did then, evangelization today also demands total and faithful adherence to God's Word: adherence to Christ first of all and attentive listening to his Spirit who guides the Church, docile obedience to the pastors whom God has chosen to guide his people and prudent, frank dialogue with the social, cultural and religious bodies of our time. All this presupposes, as is well known, close communion with the one who calls us to be his friends and disciples, a unity of life and action nourished by listening to his Word, by contemplation and by prayer, by detachment from the mindset of the world and by ceaseless conversion to his love so that it may be he, Christ, who lives and works in each one of us. Here lies the secret of the authentic success of every Christian's apostolic and missionary commitment, and especially of those who are called to a more direct service of the gospel.

3. This awareness is certainly vividly present to those who are taking part in the General Congregation, and I am eager to pay a tribute to the important work carried out by the Preparatory Commission which, in the course of 2007, examined the proposals submitted by the Provinces and pointed out the themes to address. I would like, in the first place, to address my grateful thoughts to you, dear and venerable Father General, who has guided the Society of Jesus since 1983 with enlightenment, wisdom and prudence, leaving no stone unturned to keep it in the channel of its original charism. For objective reasons, you have asked on

[2] 1 Thessalonians 2:13.

several occasions to be relieved of this heavy burden, assumed with a great sense of responsibility during a period in the Order's history that was far from easy. I express my warmest gratitude to you for your service to the Society of Jesus and, more generally, to the Church. I extend my sentiments of gratitude to your closest collaborators, to the participants in the General Congregation and to all the Jesuits scattered in every part of the globe. May the greeting of the Successor of Peter reach each and every one; he follows with affection and esteem the multifaceted and appreciated apostolic work of the Jesuits and encourages them all to continue on the path plotted by the Holy Founder and trodden by an innumerable array of brothers dedicated to Christ's cause, many of whom the Church has inscribed in the roll of Blesseds and Saints. May they, from heaven, protect and support the Society of Jesus in the mission it is carrying out in our time, marked by many complex social, cultural and religious challenges.

4. Moreover, precisely in this regard, how can we fail to recognise the valid contribution the Society offers to the Church's action in various fields and in many ways? It is a truly great and praiseworthy contribution which only the Lord will be able to reward as it deserves! Like my venerable Predecessors, the Servants of God Paul VI and John Paul II, I also willingly take the opportunity afforded by the General Congregation to shed light on this contribution, and at the same time to offer for your reflection certain considerations which may be an encouragement and incentive to bring to fruition in an ever better way the ideal of the Society, in total fidelity to the Church's Magisterium, as has been described in the following formula with which you are well acquainted:

> To serve as a soldier of God beneath the banner of the Cross and to serve the Lord alone and the Church, his

spouse, under the Roman Pontiff, the Vicar of Christ on earth.[3]

This is a 'particular' fidelity, sanctioned for many of you by a vow of immediate obedience to the Successor of Peter '*perinde ac cadaver*'. Today, the Church is still particularly in need of this fidelity of yours which constitutes the badge of your Order, in an age when the urgent need is felt to pass on in its integral form to our contemporaries, who are distracted by so many discordant voices, the one, unchanged message of salvation which is the gospel, 'not as the word of men, but as it truly is, as the Word of God',[4] which is at work in you believers.

5. If this is to happen, it is indispensable for the life of members of the Society of Jesus and their doctrinal research, as beloved John Paul II formerly reminded the participants in the 34th General Congregation, to be animated by a true spirit of faith and communion, always in 'humble fidelity to the teachings of the Magisterium'.[5] I warmly hope that this Congregation will clearly reaffirm the authentic charism of the Founder in order to encourage all Jesuits to promote true, sound Catholic doctrine. As Prefect of the Congregation for the Doctrine of the Faith, I have had the opportunity to appreciate the effective collaboration of Jesuit Consultors and experts who, in full fidelity to their charism, have made a considerable contribution to the faithful promotion and reception of the Magisterium. This is not, of course, a simple task, especially when one is called to proclaim the gospel in very different social and cultural contexts and is obliged to address different mindsets. Thus, I sincerely appreciate this effort dedicated to serving Christ, an endeavour which is fruitful for the

[3] Formula of the Institute, *Constitutions*, 1.

[4] 1 Thessalonians 2: 13.

[5] John Paul II, allocution, GC 34, appendix I, § 5.

true good of souls to the extent that they allow themselves to be guided by the Holy Spirit and in humble fidelity to the teachings of the Magisterium, referring to those key principles of the Instruction on the Ecclesial Vocation of the Theologian outlined in *Donum veritatis* (24 May 1990).

6. The Church's evangelizing work therefore relies heavily on the Society's responsibility for formation in the fields of theology, spirituality and mission. And precisely in order to offer the entire Society of Jesus clear guidelines to support its generous and faithful apostolic dedication, it might prove particularly useful for the Congregation to reassert, in the spirit of St Ignatius, its own total adherence to Catholic doctrine, especially to its key points, under severe attack today by the secular culture, such as, for example, the relationship between Christ and religions, certain aspects of liberation theology and the various points of sexual morals, especially those concerning the indissolubility of marriage and the pastoral care of homosexuals. Reverend and dear Father, I am convinced that the Society senses the historic importance of this General Congregation and, guided by the Holy Spirit, desires once again, as beloved John Paul II said in January 1995, to reaffirm 'unequivocally and without any hesitation its specific way to God, which St Ignatius sketched out in the Formula of the Institute: loving fidelity to your charism will be the certain source of renewed effectiveness'.[6] Furthermore, how timely were my venerable Predecessor Paul VI's words on a similar occasion:

> All of us must be vigilant so that the necessary adaptation will not be accomplished to the detriment of the fundamental identity or essential character of the role of the Jesuit as is described in the *Formula instituti* as the history and particular spirituality of the Order

[6] John Paul II, allocution, GC 34, appendix I, § 3.

> propose it, and as the authentic interpretation of the very needs of the times seem still to require it. This image must not be altered; it must not be distorted.[7]

8. The continuity of the teachings of the Successors of Peter demonstrates the great attention and care that they show for the Jesuits, their esteem for you and their desire always to be able to count on the Society's precious contribution to the life of the Church and to the evangelization of the world.

I entrust the General Congregation and the entire Society of Jesus to the intercession of the Holy Founder and the Saints of the Order and to Mary's maternal protection, so that every spiritual son of St Ignatius may have before his eyes 'first of all ... God and then the nature of this his Institute'.[8] With such sentiments, I assure you of a constant remembrance in prayer and in a heartfelt way I impart to you, Reverend Father, and to the Fathers of the General Congregation and to the entire Society of Jesus, a special Apostolic Blessing.

Vatican, 10 January 2008
Benedict PP XVI

(original in Italian)

7 Paul VI, allocution, GC 32, II, § 10.

8 Formula of the Institute, *Constitutions*, 1.

2. Allocution of His Holiness Benedict XVI to the 35th General Congregation of the Society of Jesus, 21 February 2008

Dear Fathers of the General Congregation of the Society of Jesus,

1. I am pleased to welcome you today as your demanding work is reaching its conclusion. I thank the new Superior General, Fr Adolfo Nicolás, for expressing your sentiments and your commitment to respond to the expectations that the Church has of you. I spoke to you of this in the message I addressed to Reverend Father Kolvenbach and—through him—to the entire Congregation at the beginning of its work. I once again thank Fr Peter-Hans Kolvenbach for the valuable service he has rendered to your Order in governing it for almost a quarter of a century. I also greet the members of the new General Council and the Assistants who will help the Superior General in his most delicate task as the religious and apostolic guide of your entire Society.

2. Your Congregation is being held during a period of great social, economic and political change; of conspicuous ethical, cultural and environmental problems, of conflicts of all kinds; yet also of more intense communication between peoples, of new possibilities for knowledge and dialogue, of profound aspirations for peace. These are situations that deeply challenge the Catholic Church and her capacity for proclaiming to our contemporaries the Word of hope and salvation. I therefore ardently hope that, thanks to the results of your Congregation, the entire Society of Jesus will be able to live out with renewed dynamism and fervour the mission for which the Spirit willed it in the Church and has preserved it for more than four and a half centuries with extraordinary apostolic

fruitfulness. Today, in the ecclesial and social context that marks the beginning of this millennium, I would like to encourage you and your confrères to continue on the path of this mission in full fidelity to your original charism. As my Predecessors have said to you on various occasions, the Church needs you, relies on you and continues to turn to you with trust, particularly to reach those physical and spiritual places which others do not reach or have difficulty in reaching. Paul VI's words remain engraved on your hearts:

> Wherever in the Church, even in the most difficult and extreme fields, at the crossroads of ideologies, in the social trenches, there has been and there is confrontation between the burning exigencies of man and the perennial message of the Gospel, here also there have been, and there are, Jesuits.[9]

3. As the Formula of your Institute says, the Society of Jesus was founded in the first place 'for the defence and propagation of the faith'. In an age when new geographical horizons were unfolding, Ignatius' First Companions placed themselves at the Pope's disposal so that 'he might employ them wherever he judged to be more for the glory of God and the good of souls'.[10] Thus, they were sent to proclaim the Lord to peoples and cultures that did not yet know him. They did so with a courage and zeal that have lived on to our day as an exemplary inspiration. The name of Francis Xavier is the most famous of all, but how many others one could give! The new peoples, who do not know the Lord or who do not know him well so that they cannot recognise him as the Saviour, are distant today not so much from the geographical as rather from the cultural viewpoint. It is not oceans or immense distances that

9 Paul VI, allocution, II, § 8.

10 *Autobiography*, 85.

challenge the heralds of the gospel but the boundaries resulting from an erroneous or superficial vision of God and man that stand between faith and human knowledge, faith and modern science, faith and the commitment to justice.

4. The Church thus urgently needs people with a deep and sound faith, a well-grounded culture and genuine human and social sensitivity, of religious and priests who dedicate their lives to being on these very frontiers to bear witness and to help people understand that on the contrary there is profound harmony between faith and reason, between the gospel spirit, the thirst for justice and initiatives for peace. Only in this way will it be possible to make the Lord's true Face known to the many for whom he is still concealed or unrecognisable. The Society of Jesus should therefore give preferential attention to this. Faithful to its best tradition, it must persevere in taking great pains to form its members in knowledge and virtue and not to be content with mediocrity, since confrontation and dialogue with the very different social and cultural contexts and the diverse mentalities of today's world is one of the most difficult and demanding tasks. This quest for quality and for human, spiritual and cultural validity must also characterize the whole of the Jesuits' many-faceted formative and educative activities as they come into contact with people of every sort wherever they may happen to be.

5. In its history, the Society of Jesus has lived extraordinary experiences of proclamation and encounter between the gospel and world cultures—it suffices to think of Matteo Ricci in China, Roberto De Nobili in India or of the 'Reductions' in Latin America. And you are rightly proud of them. I feel it is my duty today to urge you to set out once again in the tracks of your predecessors with the same courage and intelligence, but

also with an equally profound motivation of faith and enthusiasm to serve the Lord and his Church. However, while you seek to recognise the signs of God's presence and work in every corner of the world, even beyond the bounds of the visible Church, while you strive to build bridges of understanding and dialogue with those who do not belong to the Church or have difficulty in accepting her outlook or messages, at the same time you must loyally take on the Church's fundamental duty to remain faithful to her mandate and to adhere totally to the Word of God and to the Magisterium's task of preserving the integral truth and unity of Catholic doctrine. This not only applies to the personal commitment of individual Jesuits: since you are working as members of an apostolic body, you must also take care that your work and institutions always maintain a clear and explicit identity, so that the goal of your apostolic activity is neither ambiguous nor obscure and that many others may share in your ideals and join you effectively and enthusiastically, collaborating in your commitment to serve God and man.

6. As you are well aware, since in the Spiritual Exercises you have often undertaken meditation on 'the two flags' under St Ignatius' guidance, our world is the theatre of a battle between good and evil where powerful negative forces are at work. These are what cause the dramatic situations of spiritual and material enslavement of our contemporaries which you have several times declared you wished to combat, committing yourselves to the service of faith and the promotion of justice. These forces are manifest today in many ways but are especially evident in such overriding cultural trends as subjectivism, relativism, hedonism and practical materialism. This is the reason why I asked you for a renewed commitment to promoting and defending Catholic doctrine, 'especially ...

its key points, under severe attack today by the secular culture' of which I gave some examples in my letter.[11] The themes, continuously discussed and called into question today, of the salvation of all humanity in Christ, of sexual morality, of marriage and the family, must be explored and illumined in the context of contemporary reality but preserving that harmony with the Magisterium which avoids causing confusion and dismay among the People of God.

7. I know and understand well that this is a particularly sensitive and demanding point for you and for some of your confrères, especially those involved in theological research, interreligious dialogue and dialogue with contemporary cultures. For this very reason I have invited you and also invite you today to reflect in order to rediscover the fullest meaning of your characteristic 'Fourth Vow' of obedience to the Successor of Peter, which does not only involve the readiness to be sent on mission to distant lands but also—in the most genuine Ignatian spirit of 'feeling with the Church and in the Church'—'to love and serve' the Vicar of Christ on earth with that 'effective and affective devotion' which must make you his invaluable and irreplaceable collaborators in his service for the universal Church.

8. At the same time, I encourage you to continue and to renew your mission among the poor and with the poor. Unfortunately, new causes of poverty and marginalisation are not absent in a world marked by grave financial and environmental imbalances, from globalisation processes prompted by selfishness rather than solidarity and by devastating and senseless armed conflicts. As I was able to reaffirm to the Latin American Bishops gathered at the Shrine of Aparecida, 'the preferential option for the poor is implicit in the Christological faith in the God who

[11] Benedict XVI, letter, § 6.

became poor for us, so as to enrich us with his poverty (cf. 2 Corinthians 8:9)'.[12] It is therefore natural that those who truly want to be a companion of Jesus really share in his love for the poor. For us, the option for the poor is not ideological but is born from the gospel. Situations of injustice and poverty in today's world are numerous and tragic, and if it is necessary to seek to understand them and fight their structural causes, it is also necessary to penetrate to the very heart of man, to extirpate the deep roots of evil and sin that cut him off from God, without forgetting to meet people's most urgent needs in the spirit of Christ's charity. Gathering and developing one of Fr Arrupe's last far-sighted intuitions, your Society continues to do praiseworthy work in the service for refugees, who are often the poorest of the poor and in need not only of material aid but also of the deeper spiritual, human and psychological closeness that is very much a part of your service.

9. Lastly, I ask you to focus special attention on that ministry of Spiritual Exercises which has been a characteristic feature of your Society from the outset. The Exercises are not only the source of your spirituality and the matrix of your *Constitutions* but also a gift which the Spirit of the Lord has made to the entire Church. It is your task to continue to make them a valuable and effective means for the spiritual growth of souls, for their initiation to prayer, to meditation in this secularised world where God seems to be absent. Only last week I myself benefited from the Spiritual Exercises, together with my closest collaborators of the Roman Curia, under the guidance of a distinguished confrère of yours, Cardinal Albert Vanhoye. In a time like ours, when the confusion and multiplicity of messages and the speed of changes and situations make it

[12] Benedict XVI, address to the 5th General Conference of the Bishops of Latin America, 13 May 2007, 3. § 9.

particularly difficult for our contemporaries to put order into their lives and respond with determination and joy to the call the Lord addresses to each one of us, the Spiritual Exercises are a particularly precious means and method with which to seek God, within us, around us and in all things, to know his will and to put it into practice.

10. In this spirit of obedience to God's will, to Jesus Christ, which also becomes humble obedience to the Church, I ask you to continue carrying out your Congregation's work and I join you in the prayer St Ignatius taught us at the end of the Exercises—a prayer which to me always seems too sublime in the sense that I hardly dare to say it, yet we must always be able to return to it:

> Take, Lord, and receive all my liberty, my memory, my understanding and all my will—all that I have and possess. You, Lord, have given all that to me. I now give it back to you, O Lord. All of it is yours. Dispose of it according to your will. Give me love of yourself and your grace, for that is enough for me.[13]

(original in Italian)

[13] Exx, 234.

Father General

3. Fr Kolvenbach to the Society, on the Pope's Response

Curia Generalizia della Compagnia di Gesù
Borgo S. Spirito, 4
C.Fr 6139 00195 ROMA-PRATI (Italia)
Tel . 06/689.771—Fax 06/686.8214

The Holy Father's response
2007/03

TO ALL MAJOR SUPERIORS AND ELECTORS OF **GC 35**

Dear Fathers,

As material for your meetings and discussions in preparation for the 35th General Congregation, I would like to share with you a decision and a desire that the Holy Father recently communicated to me.

In accord with our *Constitutions*, last 24 January I submitted to the Holy Father the issue about whether or not to maintain the *ad vitam* mandate of the Superior General of the Society. This issue had been discussed previously by the commission on juridical matters in preparation for the General Congregation.

In his response of January 29, the Holy Father determined that the term of the Superior General remain *ad vitam,* while maintaining the General's right to resign in special cases after having first informed the Holy Father of his intention. The Holy Father's agreement then allows the whole process laid out in the *Constitutions* and the *Complementary Norms* for the convocation of a General Congregation *ad electionem* to begin. Thus the Holy Father has confirmed the present practice.

Furthermore, the Holy Father expressed the desire that the General Congregation reflect on the spiritual and ecclesial formation of young Jesuits, and also on the value and observance of the Fourth Vow for the whole Society. The Holy Father had already mentioned this concern in his address to the Society in the Basilica of St Peter on 22 April 2006. The commission that is preparing a document on obedience in the Society will give this deeply Ignatian characteristic of our apostolic commitment its due importance. It merits our attention during this time of preparation. The Society, in effect, completely submits its judgment and its will to Christ Our Lord and to his Vicar (cf. *Constitutions*, VII.1.2. [606]).

I assure you of my union of prayer and of work in the preparation for the upcoming General Congregation.

Fraternally yours in the Lord,

Peter-Hans Kolvenbach sj.

Peter-Hans Kolvenbach SJ, Superior General
Rome, 21 February 2007

(original in French)

4. Fr Kolvenbach's Initial Answer to the Pope

Curia Generalizia della Compagnia di Gesù
Borgo S. Spirito, 4
C.Fr 6139 00195 ROMA-PRATI (Italia)
Tel . 06/689.771—Fax 06/686.8214

HIS HOLINESS BENEDICT XVI
Vatican City
Rome

15 January 2008

Most Holy Father,

The General Congregation has received with profound attention and gratitude the message that His Holiness, Pope Benedict XVI, has addressed to the Superior General and—through him—to the whole Society of Jesus during this meaningful and important moment in the life of our Order.

The Holy Father has manifested once again the affection, spiritual closeness, esteem and gratitude with which the Successors of Peter have regarded and see the Society of Jesus, continuing to expect the faithful service of the Society for the integral and clear proclamation of the gospel in our time. While the Holy Father confirms that the intimate union with Christ should be the secret of our apostolic and missionary life, he recalls the original charism of the Society of Jesus as defined in the Formula of the Institute: 'to serve as a soldier of God beneath the banner of the Cross ... and to serve the Lord alone and the Church, his spouse, under the Roman Pontiff, the Vicar of Christ on earth'.

In continuity with the interventions of his predecessors—in particular Pope Paul VI and Pope John Paul II, on the occasion of the previous General Congregations—and with his other previous interventions, the Holy Father recalls the particular bond that binds the Society of Jesus to the Successor of Peter, as expressed in the Fourth Vow of special obedience to the Pope. The Holy Father underlines 'the formative responsibility of the Society in the fields of theology, spirituality and mission', asking that 'the General Congregation reaffirm, in the spirit of St Ignatius, its own total adhesion to Catholic doctrine, especially in its key points, under severe attack today by the secular culture', examples of which he mentions explicitly.

The Society of Jesus affirms its own desire to respond sincerely to the call and demands of the Holy Father. The General Congregation will give them full attention in the course of its labours, a considerable part of which will be dedicated exactly on the topics of the identity and mission of the Jesuits, and on religious and apostolic obedience, in particular obedience to the Holy Father.

The Congregation has set out to face its tasks with confidence and serenity, knowing that it can count on the affection and prayer of the Holy Father and his deep understanding of the difficult challenge 'to announce the gospel in the various social and cultural contexts, being confronted with different mentalities', as the mission the Society of Jesus demands today for the service of the Church.

With profound gratitude, devotedly yours in the Lord,

Peter-Hans Kolvenbach sj.

Peter-Hans Kolvenbach SJ

(original in Italian)

5. Fr Nicolás to Benedict XVI: Special Audience, 21 February 2008

On 21 February at 11:30, the members of the General Congregation were received by the Holy Father Benedict XVI in a special audience. Before the Pope's discourse, Father General pronounced the following words:

Most Holy Father,

I would like my first word to be, in my name and in the name of all present, a heartfelt 'thank you' to Your Holiness for kindly receiving today the members of the General Congregation meeting in Rome, after having already bestowed on us the precious gift of a letter which, by way of its rich content and its positive tone, encouraging and affectionate, has most surely been appreciated by the whole Society of Jesus.

Gratitude, indeed, and a strong sense of communion in feeling confirmed in our mission to work at the frontiers where faith and science, faith and justice, and faith and knowledge confront each other, and in the challenging field of serious reflection and responsible theological research. We are grateful to Your Holiness to have been once more encouraged to follow our Ignatian tradition of service right where the gospel and the Church suffer the greatest challenges, a service which at times also lends itself to the risk of disturbing a peaceful lifestyle, reputation and security. For us it is a cause of great consolation to note that Your Holiness is more than aware of the dangers that such a commitment exposes to us.

Holy Father, I would like to return once again to the kind and generous letter which you sent to my predecessor, Fr Kolvenbach, and through him to all of us. We have received it with an open heart, meditated on it, reflected on it, we have exchanged our reflections, and we are determined to carry its message and its unconditional words of welcome and acceptance to the whole Society of Jesus.

We wish moreover to convey the spirit of such a message to all our formation structures and to create—taking the message as our starting point—opportunities for reflection and discussion which will enable us to assist our confrères engaged in research and in service.

Our General Congregation, to which Your Holiness has given Your paternal encouragement, is looking, in prayer and in discernment, for the ways through which the Society can renew its commitment to the service of the Church and of humanity.

What inspires and impels us is the gospel and the Spirit of Christ: if the Lord Jesus was not at the centre of our life we would have no sense of our apostolic activity, we would have no reason for our existence. It is from the Lord Jesus we learn to be near to the poor and suffering, to those who are excluded in this world.

The spirituality of the Society of Jesus has as its source the Spiritual Exercises of St Ignatius. And it is in the light of the Spiritual Exercises—which in their turn inspired the *Constitutions* of the Society—that the General Congregation is in these days tackling the subjects of our identity and of our mission. The Spiritual Exercises, before becoming a precious tool for the apostolate, are for the Jesuit the touchstone by which to judge our own spiritual maturity.

In communion with the Church and guided by the Magisterium, we seek to dedicate ourselves to profound service, to discernment, to research. The generosity with which so many Jesuits work for the Kingdom of God, even to giving their very lives for the Church, does not mitigate the sense of responsibility that the Society feels it has in the Church. Responsibility that Your Holiness confirms in Your letter, when You affirm: 'The Church's evangelizing work therefore relies heavily on the Society's responsibility for formation in the fields of theology, spirituality and mission'.[1]

Alongside the sense of responsibility, must go humility, recognising that the mystery of God and of man is much greater than our capacity for understanding.

It saddens us, Holy Father, when the inevitable deficiencies and superficialities of some among us are at times used to dramatize and represent as conflicts and clashes what are often only manifestations of limits and human imperfections, or inevitable tensions, of everyday life. But all this does not discourage us, nor quell our passion, not only to serve the Church, but also, with a deeper sense of our roots, according to the spirit of the Ignatian tradition, to love the hierarchical Church and the Holy Father, the Vicar of Christ.

'*En todo amar y servir.*' This represents a portrait of who Ignatius is. This is the identity card of a true Jesuit.

And so we consider it a happy and significant circumstance that our meeting with You occurs on this particular day, the vigil of the Feast of the Chair of St Peter, a day of prayer and of union with the Pope and His highest service of universal teaching authority. For this we offer You our good wishes. And now, Holy Father, we are ready and willing, to listen and attend to what You have to say to us.

(original in Italian)

1 Benedict XVI, letter, § 6.

6. Fr Nicolás' First Letter to the Whole Society

Curia Generalizia della Compagnia di Gesù
Borgo S. Spirito, 4
C.Fr 6139 00195 ROMA-PRATI (Italia)
Tel . 06/689.771—Fax 06/686.8214

First Greetings
2008/05
To The Whole Society

Dear Friends in the Lord,

This is the first time I write to you since the election, exactly one month ago, on 19 January. I think you can easily imagine the surprise, even shock, I received with the election. I had considered myself out of bounds because of my age, without entering into the long series of inadequacies and shortcomings that are well known to those with whom I have lived and worked.

Maybe the most difficult thing to explain is the experience we all went through on those days, searching in the fog, looking for the Will of God and the good of the Church and the Society. It was this intense, sincere and open search that made it impossible for me to decline or refuse the choice. You cannot say 'no' to people so sincerely looking for the Will of God. And now I assure you that I will give all my energy and person to the work of helping the Society move forward, supporting what is good, responding to new challenges, encouraging to face the difficult task of being consistent with and credible witnesses of the gospel of Jesus Christ that we believe in.

The task is daunting, the service needed is unlimited, the pace of change in our world is dizzying; we could not even dream of contributing to the mission of our Society if the Lord were not with us, guiding, supporting and comforting us with his Spirit. We will be led and supported by this Spirit and the love for the Church in all its different manifestations. We want to serve this Church with total dedication and depth under the guidance of and in fidelity to the Holy Father, and in an ever friendly and trusting cooperation with the hierarchy wherever we are.

The incredible support, availability and spirit of service that I am finding in the General Congregation and at all levels of this Roman Curia is a source of joy and of hope. This convinces me that we Jesuits will be able to continue doing our best for others; and that we will take our humble position in the Church, as servants called to share our lives, invited to teach and to learn, to search for depth and to pray with intensity and joy.

The weeks following the election have been equally intensive in the search of a good team to help me with the governance of the Society. We have almost concluded the task with the election of the four Assistants *ad providentiam* and the Admonitor. I am deeply grateful to the General Congregation; they have given me an excellent team that will help me sleep better, with the confidence that I have the best possible advice and support. Even so I will probably make mistakes and will need your understanding and forgiveness whenever they happen. Be 'generously' ready!

As you have surely read elsewhere, the new group of Regional Assistants and General Councillors is composed of the following men:

Africa—Fr Jean-Roger Ndombi (AOC)

South Latin America—Fr Marcos Recolons (BOL)

North Latin America—Fr Gabriel Ignacio Rodríguez (COL)

South Asia—Fr Lisbert D'Souza (BOM)

East Asia and Oceania—Fr Daniel Huang (PHI)

Central and East Europe—Fr Adam Żak (PME)

South Europe—Fr Joaquín Barrero Díaz (CAS)

West Europe—Fr Antoine Kerhuel (GAL)

United States—Fr James E. Grummer (WIS)

I have also named two General Councillors who will normally reside outside Rome and come to Rome as needed. They are:

Fr Mark Rotsaert (BSE and CEP)

Fr Arturo M. Sosa Abascal (VEN)

The four Assistants *ad providentiam* elected on Monday, 18 February are:

Fr Lisbert D'Souza

Fr James E. Grummer

Fr Federico Lombardi (ITA)

Fr Marcos Recolons

Also on 18 February I named Fr Ignacio Echarte (LOY) the new Secretary of the Society, to succeed Fr Frank E. Case (ORE).

It is my pleasure to take this occasion to thank, on behalf of the entire Society, all who will soon be leaving the General Curia after the General Congregation. First of all, we all owe a deep and sincere vote of thanks to Fr Peter-Hans Kolvenbach for his tireless, inspiring and very wise leadership of the Society over the past quarter of a century. Likewise I want to thank the outgoing General Councillors—Frs Joseph Nguyên Công Đoan (ASO and VIE), Jacques Gellard (EOC and GAL), Jean Ilboudo (AFR and AOC), Wendelin Köster (ECE and GER), Valentín Menéndez (ALS and CAM), Manuel Morujão (EMR and POR) and Ignacio Echarte (DIR and LOY)—and Fr Frank Case, the outgoing Secretary of the Society. They have served the Church and the Society generously and well.

Other changes will be taking place in the Curia after the Congregation, of which I will be informing you in due time.

Finally, while counting on the accompaniment of your prayers during the coming months of transition, I also commend the remaining days of the General Congregation to your continued good prayers.

Sincerely in the Lord,

A. Nicolás SJ

A. Nicolás SJ
Superior General
Rome, 22 February 2008

Resignation of Fr Kolvenbach

7. Fr Menéndez: The General Congregation's Words of Gratitude to Fr Kolvenbach

CG35

Now that General Congregation 35 has accepted your resignation, it is fitting that this same Congregation gathered here today express, in the whole Society's name, its profound gratitude to you for your crucial service, as missioned by the Lord, to the Church and to the Society.

First of all, we wish to tell you how edified we are with your manner of submitting your resignation, namely, in that freedom of spirit that frames the gospel and the Exercises. The example you give us today, of course, is very different from what commonly is found in a world characterized by the clinging to, and fighting for, positions of power and prestige. Our charism and legislation are not good merely because they propose beautiful ideals, but precisely because there are people who know how to embody and live them.

We are most especially grateful to you for the way in which you governed the Society following the difficult 1981 pontifical intervention. Since then, you have known how to navigate the Society with serenity, recognising how to balance fidelity to the Church with fidelity to our way of proceeding as expressed in our *Constitutions* and the most recent General Congregations. The words we heard in Cardinal Rodé's homily, which represent the thinking of the Church, clearly express the Holy See's esteem for you and your leadership during these past years.

We also appreciate the charism of union that you and your governance have represented for us, especially in light of the Society's ever greater plurality and cultural diversity. While living that freedom of spirit typical of our manner of proceeding and in the midst of cultural diversity, of varied ways of feeling and thinking, and through different historical contexts, you have maintained the union of the Society's corporate body. You have kept that union by being respectful of others, by means of your wise and balanced counsel, and by your inspiring presence in every Province.

The trust that you have shown through your governance, not only to your curial staff but also to all of the Provincials, has created a fraternal and collaborative setting. This broad setting has indeed affected the entire body of the Society and expresses very well one of our ideals, namely, to be, all of us together, companions of Jesus.

May our Creator and Lord reward you for your faithful service during nearly a quarter of a century. Additionally, we ask that the Lord continue to bless you in whatever new ministry he grants you for his greater glory.

In GC 35's name and that of the whole Society, and with all of our heart, we say: thank you very much, Fr Kolvenbach! We are proud of you and of your service during these difficult but exciting years the Lord has seen fit to give us.

Rome, 14 January 2008

8. Fr Kolvenbach to the Society, 14 January 2008

Curia Generalizia della Compagnia di Gesù
Borgo S. Spirito, 4
C.Fr 6139 00195 ROMA-PRATI (Italia)
Tel. 06/689.771—Fax 06/686.8214

Dear Fathers and Brothers,

Today the General Congregation has thought it well to accept my resignation as Superior General of the Society of Jesus. At the end of these nearly 25 years of service, I want first of all to thank the Lord, who—to use the words of St Ignatius—has truly been propitious to me at Rome, in leading a Society he has called into service for his greater glory.

I am also most grateful for the privilege of having met and accompanied so many friends in the Lord, who in their many diverse vocations have always shown themselves to be true servants of the Mission of Christ.

No single Jesuit should feel himself excluded from this profound sentiment of recognition. Nonetheless I would like to thank in a particular way those in the General Curia who have helped me day after day over many years in carrying out my responsibilities for the Society, as well as all the Major Superiors spread throughout the entire world.

Earlier I was able to express my great thanks to the Holy Father for his apostolic orientations which have allowed the Society to continue our mission 'under the banner of the Cross and under the Vicar of Christ on earth'.

Let us be grateful to the Lord that, despite a disconcerting diversity of persons and cultures, of desires and works, our union of minds and hearts has never failed, and, despite an increasing fragility, the Society retains the capacity of apostolic dialogue before the challenges of the modern world in proclaiming the one good news.

On this eve of the election of my successor and of the many decisions that the General Congregation will have to make, I unite myself with the prayer with which St Ignatius finished his letters: 'May God our Lord in his infinite and supreme goodness be pleased to give us his abundant grace, so that we may know his most holy will and entirely fulfill it'.

Fraternally yours in the Lord,

Peter-Hans Kolvenbach sj.

Peter-Hans Kolvenbach SJ
Rome, 14 January 2008

(original in French)

Homilies

9. Cardinal Rodé: Opening Mass, 7 January 2008

Dear members of the 35th General Congregation of the Society of Jesus,

St Ignatius considered the General Congregation 'work and [a] distraction'[1] which momentarily interrupts the apostolic commitments of a large number of qualified members of the Society of Jesus and, for this reason, clearly differing from what is customary in other religious Institutes, the *Constitutions* establish that it should be celebrated at determined times and not too often.

Nevertheless, it must be called principally on two occasions: for the election of the Superior General and when things of particular importance or very difficult problems which touch the body of the Society must be treated.

This is the second time in the history of the Society when a General Congregation has gathered to elect a new Superior General while his predecessor is still living. The first time was in 1983, when the 33rd General Congregation accepted the resignation of the much loved Fr Arrupe, for whom the exercising of the role of governance had become impossible owing to a serious and unforeseen illness. Today it gathers a second time, to discern, before the Lord, the resignation presented by Fr Kolvenbach, who has directed the Society for nearly 25 years with wisdom, prudence, commitment and loyalty. This will be followed by the election of his successor. I wish to express to you, Fr Kolvenbach, in my name and in the name of the

1 *Constitutions*, VIII. 2.1. [677].

Church, a heartfelt thanks for your fidelity, your wisdom, your righteousness and your example of humility and poverty. Thank you, Fr Kolvenbach.

The election of a new Superior General of the Society of Jesus has a fundamental value for the life of the Society, not only because its centralised hierarchical structure constitutionally concedes to the General full authority for good governance and the conservation and growth of the whole Society, but also because, as St Ignatius says so well, 'the well-being ... of the head has its consequences in the whole body ... the subjects will be what these Superiors are'.[2] For this reason your Founder, when pointing out the qualities which the General must have, places first of all that he must be 'closely united with God our Lord and have familiarity with him in prayer'.[3] After having mentioned other important qualities which are not easily found in a single person, he ends by saying 'if any of the aforementioned qualities should be wanting, he should at least not lack great probity and love for the Society, nor good judgment'.[4]

I join you in your prayer that the Holy Spirit, the father of the poor, giver of graces and light for hearts will assist you in your discernment and your election.

This Congregation also gathers together to treat important and very difficult matters which touch all members of the Society, such as the direction which the Society is presently taking. The themes upon which the General Congregation will reflect have to do with basic elements for the life of the Society. Certainly you will deal with the identity of today's Jesuit, on the meaning and value of the vow of obedience to the Holy Father which

[2] *Constitutions*, X. 8. [820].

[3] *Constitutions*, IX. 2. 1. [723].

[4] *Constitutions*, IX. 2. 10 [735].

has always defined your religious family, the mission of the Society in the context of globalisation and marginalisation, community life, apostolic obedience, vocation recruitment and other important themes.

Within your charism and your tradition you can find valuable points of reference to enlighten the choices which the Society must make today.

Certainly and necessarily, during this Congregation you are carrying out an important work but it is not a 'distraction' from your apostolic activity. As St Ignatius teaches you in the *Spiritual Exercises*, you must with the same vision of the three Divine Persons, look at 'the whole surface ... of the world, full of people'.[5] Listening to the Spirit, the Creator who renews the world and returning to the fonts to preserve your identity without losing your own lifestyle, the commitment to discern the signs of the times, the difficulty and responsibility of working out final decisions are activities which are eminently apostolic because they form the base of a new springtime of being religious and of the apostolic commitment of each of your brothers in the Society of Jesus.

Now the vision becomes broader. It is not only for your own Jesuit brothers that you provide a religious and apostolic formation. There are many institutes of consecrated life who, following an Ignatian spirituality, pay attention to your choices; there are many future priests in your colleges and universities who are preparing for their ministry. There are many peoples from both within and outside the Church who frequent your centres of learning seeking a response to the challenges which science, technology and globalisation pose to humanity, to the Church, and to the faith, with the hope of receiving a

[5] Exx, 102.

formation which will make it possible for them to construct a world of truth and freedom, of justice and peace.

Your work must be eminently apostolic with a universal human, ecclesial and evangelical fullness. It must always be carried out in the light of your charism, in such a way that the growing participation of laity in your activities does not obscure your identity but rather enriches it with the collaboration of those who, coming from other cultures, share your style and your objectives.

Once again I join in your prayer that the Holy Spirit may accompany you in your delicate work.

As a brother who is following your works with great interest and expectation, I want to share with you 'the joys and hopes' as well as 'the sorrows and anguish'[6] which I have as a man of the Church called to exercise a difficult service in the field of consecrated life, in my role as Prefect of the Congregation for Institutes of Consecrated Life and Societies of Apostolic Life.

With pleasure and hope I see the thousands of religious who generously respond to the Lord's call and, leaving all they have behind, consecrate themselves with an undivided heart to the Lord, to be with him and to collaborate with him in his salvific desire to 'conquer the whole world … and thus to enter into the glory of my Father'.[7] It is clear that consecrated life continues to be a 'divine gift which the Church has received from the Lord',[8] and it is for this very reason that the Church wants to watch carefully over it in order that that the proper charism of each Institute might be evermore known, and, although with the necessary adaptations to respond to the present time, keep its proper identity intact for the good of the whole Church.

[6] Gaudium et spes, n. 1.

[7] Exx, 95.

[8] *Lumen gentium*, 43.

The authenticity of religious life is characterized by the following of Christ and by the exclusive consecration to him and to his Kingdom through the profession of the evangelical counsels. The Second Vatican Ecumenical Council teaches that 'this consecration will be the more perfect, in as much as the indissoluble bond of the union of Christ and his bride, the Church, is represented by firm and more stable bonds'.[9] Consecration to service to Christ cannot be separated from consecration to service to the Church. Ignatius and his First Companions considered it thus when they wrote the Formula of your Institute in which the essence of your charism is spelled out: 'to serve the Lord alone and the Church, his spouse, under the Roman Pontiff'.[10] It is with sorrow and anxiety that I see that the *sentire cum Ecclesia* of which your Founder frequently spoke is diminishing even in some members of religious families. The Church is waiting for a light from you to restore the *sensus Ecclesiae.* The Spiritual Exercises of St Ignatius are your speciality. The rules of *sentire cum Ecclesiae* form an integral and essential part of this masterpiece of Catholic spirituality. They form, as it were, a golden clasp which holds the book of the *Spiritual Exercises* closed.

You hold in your very hands the elements needed to realise and to deepen this desire, this Ignatian and ecclesial sentiment.

Love for the Church in every sense of the word—be it the Church as the people of God, be it the hierarchical Church—is not a human sentiment which comes and goes according to the people who make it up or according to our conformity with the dispositions emanating from those whom the Lord has placed to direct the Church. Love for

9 *Lumen gentium*, 44.

10 Formula of the Institute, *Constitutions*, 1.

the Church is a love based on faith, a gift of the Lord which, precisely because he loves us, he gives us: faith in him and in his spouse, which is the Church. Without the gift of faith in the Church there can be no love for the Church.

I join in your prayer asking the Lord to grant you the grace to grow in your belief in and love for this holy, catholic and apostolic Church which we profess.

With sadness and anxiety I also see a growing distancing from the hierarchy. The Ignatian spirituality of apostolic service 'under the Roman Pontiff' does not allow for this separation. In the *Constitutions* which he left you, Ignatius wanted truly to shape your mind and, in the book of the *Exercises*, he wrote: 'we ought to keep our minds disposed and ready to be obedient in everything to the true Spouse of Christ and our Lord, which is our holy Mother the hierarchical Church'.[11] Religious obedience can be understood only as obedience in love. The fundamental nucleus of Ignatian spirituality consists in uniting the love for God with love for the hierarchical Church. Your 33rd Congregation once again took up this characteristic of obedience declaring that 'the Society reaffirms in a spirit of faith the traditional bond of love and of service which unites it to the Roman Pontiff'.[12] You returned to this principle in the motto: 'love and serve ... in all things'.[13]

You must also place this 35th General Congregation, which opens with this liturgy, celebrated close to the remains of your Founder, in this line, which has always been followed by the Society throughout its multi-century history, in order to show your desire and your commitment to be faithful to the charism, which St Ignatius left

[11] Exx, 353.

[12] GC 33, n. 7.

[13] Exx 233.

you as an inheritance, and to carry it out in ways which better respond to the needs of the Church in our time.

The service of the Society is a service 'under the banner of the cross'.[14] Every service done out of love necessarily implies a self-emptying, a *kenosis.* But letting go of what one wants to do in order to do what the beloved wants is to transform the *kenosis* into the image of Christ who *learned obedience through suffering.*[15] It is for this reason that St Ignatius, realistically, says that the Jesuit serves the Church 'under the banner of the Cross'. Ignatius placed himself under the orders of the Roman Pontiff 'to avoid erring in the path of the Lord'[16] in the distribution of his religious throughout the world and to be present wherever the needs of the Church were greater.

Times have changed and the Church must today confront new and urgent necessities, I will mention one, which in my judgment is urgent today and is at the same time complex, and I propose it for your consideration. It is the need to present to the faithful and to the world the authentic truth revealed in Scripture and Tradition. The doctrinal diversity of those who at all levels, by vocation and mission, are called to announce the Kingdom of truth and love, disorientates the faithful and leads to a relativism without limits. There is one truth, even though it can always be more deeply known. It is the 'living teaching office of the Church, whose authority is exercised in the name of Jesus Christ'[17] which is the voucher for revealed truth. The exegetes and theological scholars are involved in working together 'under the watchful care of the sacred teaching office of the Church, to an exploration and

[14] Formula of the Institute, *Constitutions*, 1.

[15] Hebrews 5: 8.

[16] *Constitutions*, VII. 1. B. [605].

[17] *Dei verbum*, 10.

exposition of the divine writings'.[18] Through your long and solid formation, your centres of research, your teaching in the philosophical-theological-biblical fields, you are in a privileged position to carry out this difficult mission. Carry it out with study and in-depth examination; carry it out with humility; carry it out with faith in the Church; carry it out with love for the Church.

May those who, according to your legislation, have to oversee the doctrine of your magazines and publications do so in the light of and according to the 'rules for *sentire cum Ecclesia*', with love and respect.

The feeling of ever growing separation between faith and culture, a separation which constitutes a great impediment for evangelization,[19] also worries me.

A culture immersed within a true Christian spirit is an instrument which fosters the spreading of the gospel, of faith in God the Creator of the heavens and of the earth. The Tradition of the Society, from the first beginnings of the Collegio Romano, always placed itself at the cross-roads between Church and society, between faith and culture, between religion and secularism. Recover these avant-garde positions which are so necessary to transmit the eternal truth to today's world, in today's language. Do not abandon this challenge. We know the task is difficult, uncomfortable and risky, and at times little appreciated and even misunderstood, but it is a necessary task for the Church. The apostolic tasks demanded of you by the Church are many and very diverse, but all have a common denominator: the instrument which carries them out, according to an Ignatian phrase, must be an instrument united to God. It is the Ignatian echo to the gospel proclaimed today: 'I am the vine, you are the branches.

[18] *Dei verbum*, 23.

[19] John Paul II, *Sapientia Cristiana,* foreword, I.

Those who abide in me and I in them bear much fruit.'[20] Union with the vine, which is love, is realised only through a personal and silent exchange of love which is born in prayer, 'from the internal knowledge of the Lord who became man for me and who, integral and alive, extends himself to all who are close to us and to all that is close to us'.[21] It is not possible to transform the world, or to respond to the challenges of a world which has forgotten love, without being firmly rooted in love.

Ignatius was granted the mystic grace of being 'a contemplative in action'.[22] It was a special grace freely given by God to Ignatius, who had trodden a tiring path of fidelity and long hours of prayer in the retreat at Manresa. It is a grace which, according to Fr Nadal, is contained in the call of every Jesuit. Guided by your Ignatian *magis*, keep your hearts open to receive the same gift, following in the same path trodden by Ignatius from Loyola to Rome: a path of generosity, of penance, of discernment, of prayer, of apostolic zeal of obedience, of charity, and of fidelity to and love for the hierarchical Church.

Despite the urgent apostolic needs, maintain and develop your charism to the point of being and showing yourselves to the world as 'contemplatives in action' who communicate to men and women and to all of creation the love received from God and orientate them once again towards the love of God. Everyone understands the language of love. The Lord has chosen you to go and bear fruit, fruit that lasts. Go, bear fruit confident that 'the Father will give you whatever you ask him in my name'.[23]

[20] John 15:5.

[21] Cf. Exx, 104.

[22] Jerónimo Nadal, 'In examen annotationes', § 31 (MHSI , 90, 162).

[23] John 15:16.

I join with you in prayer to the Father through the Son and in the Holy Spirit together with Mary, Mother of Divine Grace, invoked by all the members of the Society as *Santa Maria della Strada,* that he may grant you the grace of 'seeking and discovering the will of God for the Society of today which will build the Society of tomorrow'.

(original in Spanish)

10. Fr Frank E. Case: Mass of the Holy Spirit, 19 January 2008

These days the General Congregation, in the persons of the Electors, is passing through a moment of profound obedience on behalf of the entire Society of Jesus. It has been and will be, for many, one of the most meaningful and memorable acts of obedience of your Jesuit lives. The word 'obedience' comes from the Latin root *audire*, to hear or to listen. You have been listening to the Spirit of the Lord, both in personal prayer and in your conversations with one another. The election of a new Superior General today is a key fruit of this listening. It takes place here in Rome in the context of and in solid continuity with the Society's founding, over four and a half centuries ago, so that we might 'serve the Lord alone and the Church, his spouse, under the Roman Pontiff, the Vicar of Christ on earth'. It takes place also in the context of today's first reading, from Paul's letter to the Corinthians, describing the gifts of the Spirit to the Church we serve, gifts packaged in a variety of mixes in the men you have been considering these past four days.

In today's gospel we see Jesus, after his resurrection, breathing on his apostles, giving them the Holy Spirit for the forgiveness of sins. This Holy Spirit, whom Jesus gives, will abide in the Church to remind us of who Jesus was and of what he said and did, and to guide us in carrying his message faithfully to all the cultures and historical epochs where the gospel has been preached and is being preached today. In reminding us of who Jesus was and what he said and did, the Spirit keeps the Church faithful to her traditional roots in the revelation of God through the incarnation of his Son. The Spirit guarantees the Church's fidelity to its original inspiration and mission. In guiding us through diverse historical situations and cultures the Spirit instils the Church's mission of evangelization with a creativity that puts the gospel in words and images appropriate to so many diverse settings. This is the Church's mission under the Vicar of Christ, inspired by the Spirit.

The Spirit raised up the Society through Ignatius and his companions to serve this mission under the Vicar of Christ. Therefore what the Electors will do today, and what the Congregation will do in the following weeks, is squarely within the obedience we proclaim, an obedience of listening to the Spirit who reminds and guides, who inspires us to discern our paths in creative fidelity to our founding, as articulated in the Formula of the Institute, 'to serve as a soldier of God beneath the banner of the Cross ... and to serve the Lord alone and the Church, his spouse, under the Roman Pontiff, the Vicar of Christ on earth'. If we listen to and follow the Spirit speaking in the Church and in our Superiors, we can trust that our creativity will be faithful and our fidelity will be creative.

Besides reminding and guiding the Church in its spread of the gospel, the Spirit also holds the followers of Christ in unity with one another. For our part, in electing a Superior General today, you will give the Society a new point of union of minds and hearts and of obedience to the Spirit as servants of Christ's mission at the core of his Church.

In the words of today's Eucharist Prayer we pray the Lord: 'through the power of your Spirit of love include us now and for ever among the members of your Son, whose body and blood we share'.

11. Fr Adolfo Nicolás: Mass of Thanksgiving, Gesù Church, 20 January 2008

Above all I would like to say that this is not a message for the whole world. Rather, it is merely a simple homily; a prayerful reflection of today's readings for us Jesuits who are here this afternoon.

The first reading taken from the prophet Isaiah, briefly describes to us Christians our mission in the world. The prophet Isaiah tells us that we have all been called to serve, that we are here precisely to serve. It is a clear message regarding our mission as Jesuits, as Christians, as the people of God. God has made us servants and, in so doing, God finds delight. The Spanish version of this first reading says that God is proud of the servant, while the Italian version says that God 'is satisfied'. I believe the latter is closer to what the Bible wants to say. The more we become as servants, the more pleased God is. I think this is an image we should all take home today.

Newspapers and magazines these past few days have been toying with a number of clichés, namely, the Black Pope, the White Pope, power, gatherings, discussions .... But it is all so superficial, so artificial! These are but crumbs for those who love politics, but they are not for us.

The prophet Isaiah says that serving pleases the Lord. To serve is what counts: to serve the Church, the world, our fellow men and women, and the gospel. St Ignatius also has written in summary form about our life: in all things to love and to serve. And our Pope, Holy Father Benedict XVI, has reminded us that God is love; he has reminded us of the gospel's essence.

Later on the prophet Isaiah describes the servant's strength. God is the servant's only strength. We do not have any other source of strength: not the external strength found in politics, in business, in the media, in studies, in titles, nor the internal fortitude found in research. Only God. Exactly like the poor. Not too long ago I spoke to one of you regarding something that happened to me while working with immigrants. It was an experience that deeply affected me. A Filipina woman who had experienced many difficulties adapting to Japanese society, a woman who had suffered a great deal, was asked by another Filipina woman for advice. The second woman said, 'I have many problems with my husband and I do not know if we should get divorced or try to save our marriage .... ' In other words, she wanted advice concerning a rather common problem. The first woman replied, 'I do not know what advice to give you right now. However, come with me to Church so that the two of us can pray because only God really helps the poor.' This statement deeply touched me because it is so true. The poor only have God in whom to find their strength. For us only God is our strength. Unconditional, disinterested service finds its source of strength only in God.

The prophet Isaiah continues today's first reading by speaking about health. Our message is a message about health, about salvation. A bit later he stresses what has most caught my eye about this reading, namely, that our God, our faith, our message and our health are so great that they cannot be enclosed within a container, in any one group or community, regardless of whether or not the group in question happens to be a religious community. What is at stake is the good news of salvation for all nations. It is a universal message because the message itself is enormous; a message that in itself is irreducible.

All represented nations are gathered here today. All, everyone, is represented here. However, nations continue to open up. I ask myself today which are those 'nations'. Indeed, all geographic nations are here today. However, there may be other nations, other non-geographic communities, human communities, that claim our aid: the poor, the marginalised, the excluded. In this globalised world of ours the number of those excluded by all is increasing. Those excluded are diminished, since our society only has room for the big and not the small. All those who are disadvantaged, manipulated, all of these, may perhaps be for us those 'nations': the nations that need the prophetic message of God.

Yesterday, after the election, after the first shock, there came the moment of fraternal aid. All of you have greeted me very affectionately, offering your support and help. One of you whispered to me: 'Don't forget the poor!' Perhaps this is the most important greeting of all, just as Paul turns to the wealthier churches of his time requesting aid for the poor of Jerusalem. Don't forget the poor: These are our 'nations'. These are the nations for whom salvation is still a dream, a wish. Perhaps it may be in their midst, but they don't realise it.

And the others? The others are our collaborators, if they share our same perspective, if they have the same heart Christ has given us. And if they have a bigger heart and an even greater vision, then we are their collaborators. What counts is health, salvation, the joy of the poor. What counts, what is real, is hope, salvation, health. And we want that this salvation, this health, be an explosion of salvation that reaches out everywhere. This is what the prophet Isaiah is talking about: that salvation may reach and touch everyone. A salvation according to God's heart, will, Spirit.

We go on with our General Congregation. Perhaps this is what we need to discern. In this moment of our history where do we need to fix our attention, our service, our energy? Or, in other words, what is the colour, the tone, the image of salvation today for those many people who are in need of it, those human non-geographic nations that demand health? There are many who wait for a salvation that we have yet to understand. To open ourselves up to this reality is the challenge, the call, of the moment.

And we turn to the gospel. This is how we can be true disciples of the Lamb of God, he who takes away our sins and leads us to a new world. And he, the Lamb of God, has shown himself as Servant, he who fulfils Isaiah's prophecies, the message of the prophets. His identity as Servant will be his sign, the mark of our own mission, of the call which we try to respond to these days.

Let us pray together for this sense of Mission of the Church, that it may be for the benefit of the 'nations' and not our own. The 'nations' that are still far away, not geographically, but humanly, existentially. That the joy and the hope that come from the gospel be a reality with which we can work little by little, doing it with a lot of love and disinterested service.

(original in Italian)

12. Fr Adolfo Nicolás: Closing Mass of the 35th General Congregation, Gesù Church, 6 March 2008

I shall deliver this simple homily in Italian. I do not know whether that will put you at ease or make you uncomfortable.

Right now we are filled with the experience which we have lived for the past two months. This morning, in a prayerful and grateful spirit, we heard some reflections on this experience, an experience of incredible diversity, perhaps the greatest diversity we have ever had in the history of our General Congregations.

Along with this diversity we have experienced a strong desire to listen to others, to be open with others so different from ourselves. We have also experienced the will to change. And, yes, we have changed. We have changed in our points of view, in the drafting of our texts and in our discussions. We have developed an attitude of greater attentiveness to others. In such a large and diverse community we have rarely witnessed so much rejoicing in the joy of others and so much sadness in the suffering of others. We have prayed for one another.

The first reading of the day invites us to go to the source of this experience and to make it fully Christian. The logic of the Christian experience is very clear. God is love, and so we too love. God is mercy, and so we too show mercy. God is good, and so we too desire to be good. If we do not love, we really do not have anything to say. Here we discover, I think, the root and source of our identity and our mission. Here is our *raison d'être*. Why do we want to love the poor, to help the lonely, to console the sad, to heal the sick and to bring freedom to the oppressed? Simply because this is what God does. Nothing else. As the Holy Father told us, love for the poor does not have an ideological but a Christological basis. It is the very essence of Christ. Christ has taught us how he acts, how he lives, how God loves—and we try to learn.

Another thing which John's letter tells us is that this is not something sporadic, something we do in a fleeting moment when we feel strong, even heroic. No, it is a constant in our lives. The letter invites us to 'remain' in love. This word is repeated several times in the letter. In order for God to 'remain' in you, you must 'remain' in love. For Christ to 'remain' in you, you must be united with others. There is a play of words as the concept of 'remaining' is repeated several times.

The invitation which we have received in our Congregation and in today's liturgy is to become new persons—persons who 'remain' with our insights and who 'remain' with the contacts we have established with the Lord through one another.

In the document in which we considered our charism, we say that in looking at Jesus we understand who we ought to be. 'Remaining' in him. We all know that it is not through guidelines or directives written for others that the Church and the Society will change. They will change if we know how to become new persons. The question is not what we wish to do in community, but what kind of community men we need to become in order to 'remain' obedient men, men who know how to discern, men who are always companions, always. Not with some people whom we choose to be our collaborators, but to be companions of others always and everywhere—ready to serve, ready to offer solidarity. Men who live continually in love and in service. 'To love and to serve in all things.' How often we have sung these words in the past two months! In all things. This is not an act of heroism; it is a way of life. This is what we have prayed for these two months.

The gospel takes us still further. It tells us that everything we have done is for mission. I did not choose the gospel text for our Mass here in the Gesù. Others chose the mission of Christ as the text. At the very heart of the sending is the 'remaining'. We are sent, as you have discussed during these days and indicated in the documents. We are sent because we have entered into Christ and it is Christ who has sent us. The mission has its source, its *zampilla* as the Italians say, in our encounter with God, but it ends in others. It begins with Christ and ends with others—in their joys, in their hopes, in their sufferings. Then Mark tells us: make universal what you have experienced these two months during the General Congregation. This love and this concern for one another must now be extended to all we meet. This collaboration, this mutual help must become our way of life. This is not easy. Perhaps some of you are familiar with the power point which features letters written to Jesus by little children. One letter reads, 'Jesus, how do you manage to love everybody? There are only four of us at home and we don't do very well at loving one another.' We know what this means. At least we have accomplished it among the 225 of us. But how do we keep doing it in our local communities, in our Provinces and with our collaborators, unless we remain in love?

The gospel also indicates how we are to carry out our mission. I will limit myself to the most important points because the vision presented is very dynamic. As I have already said, it is a dynamism which begins in us when we go out to others. Something happens in others and then it is beyond us. The results are there, not here. The vision is very modern. The fruit is not 'input' but 'output'. First of all, go. Go to the whole world. We have spoken of frontiers, or the periphery. The gospel tells us: Go, go. We have indeed gone and we have encountered many problems and made many mistakes at the frontiers. I could tell you about my mistakes, but I know that there have been other mistakes as well. We have come to understand that 'going' does not mean simply getting on a plane but entering into the culture, into the life of the people. 'Going' means study, research, entering into the life of the people. Solidarity, empathy, inculturation, respect for others. Going to the whole world turns out to be more difficult than we had thought. We feel like children. Perhaps we have discovered the Kingdom of God.

We are then told: go and proclaim the gospel. We have done so—sometimes well, at other times not so well. But then we have understood that proclaiming the gospel requires that the Word of God be visible. It is not enough to proclaim it with our lips. Visibility is necessary, visibility in our life, in our work, in our openness to others, in service, in forgiveness, in compassion, in reconciliation, in our capacity to help others become healthier, freer, more human. And the gospel continues. Something happens. People have faith. Those who believe are transformed. This is where St Ignatius can be a great help to us. Ignatius saw this. Faith is not something exterior. Faith transforms. Faith is something which has happened to each one of us from the moment we became Christians, from the moment we became Jesuits. This has been a process of transformation, an all-embracing process, a process which changes the person and a process which opens the doors to hope, to love and to the risk of caring for others. When the gospel touches us, we change. Something happens and we all grow.

The gospel goes on to say that this is salvation. It is not a matter of saying, 'If I believe, I will be saved'. That is far too external. If I believe, I am already saved. To believe, to enter into this process means to find salvation. Ignatius understood this very well. This is the very essence of Ignatian pastoral practice, whether in a parish, in education or in the spirituality of our houses. Salvation consists in interior change, in interior transformation. Ignatian pastoral care, based on the Spiritual Exercises, consists precisely in helping people to change interiorly.

From this interior change of heart comes the change in feet, hands, service, work and love for others.

The end of the gospel states that there will be visible signs. These signs will be in those who believe, not in the missionary who may already have been forgotten. The centre of attention, therefore, is those whom we serve. Believers will find that their lives have been changed. The signs are the result of faith, of a life that that has been transformed. Perhaps our challenge today is to discern the signs of the gospel. Nowadays we do not handle snakes! What, then, are the signs? Justice, peace, compassion, solidarity, reconciliation and human dignity. When these have become universal, when everyone has access to these most human elements of our lives, these will be the signs. The gospel tells us that our mission is to go and proclaim the gospel which transforms the human person. The signs will follow. In yet another passage the gospel states that 'by their fruits you will know who is true and who is not'. Our question, then, must always be this: what signs do we need in our parishes, our schools, our services and all our works?

Now I conclude for today. I believe that we are all aware that we have had a great experience. The Word of God, however, invites us to go to the source of this experience and to make sure that it is being transformed into mission, an all-embracing mission, a mission which will continue to bear fruit in others. To return home with less than this cannot justify the two months we have spent together, guided by the Spirit and seeking to find God's will in all things. We pray, therefore, that this experience as well as the Word of God we have heard today will bear fruit in transforming our own lives and the lives of others, so that the faith which we communicate may always be a transforming faith. This is what I ask for all of us.

(original in Italian)

Fr Adolfo Nicolás presides at the Final Mass of the General Congregation

List of Delegates to the 35th General Congregation

Abranches, William SJ	Gujarat
Alaix Busquets, Ramón SJ	Bolivia
Álvarez de los Mozos, Francisco Javier SJ	Loyola
Alzibar Arrinda, Luis Maria SJ	Loyola
Amalraj, Paramasivam Stanislaus SJ	Andhra
Ambert, Jorge SJ	Puerto Rico
Andretta, Edson Luis SJ	Central Brazil
Anthony, Sebastian SJ	Sri Lanka
Anthonydoss, Joseph SJ	Patna
Anton, Ronald SJ	Maryland
Ariapilly, John SJ	Delhi
Arregui Echeverría, Juan SJ	Loyola
Aste, Gerardo SJ	Peru
Bafuidinsoni, Maloko-Mana SJ	Central Africa
Bambang Triatmoko, Benedictus SJ	Indonesia
Baranda, Guillermo SJ	Chile
Barla, Henry SJ	Ranchi
Barrero Díaz, Joaquín SJ	Castile
Barretta, Claudio SJ	Italy
Barros, Raimundo Oliveira SJ	North-East Brazil
Bentvelzen, Jan SJ	Netherlands
Biron, Jean-Marc SJ	French Canada
Birsens, Josy SJ	South Belgium and Luxembourg
Bisson, Peter SJ	English Canada

Borrás Durán, Pere SJ	Tarragon
Bosa, Olivo SJ	Romania
Boughton, Michael SJ	New England
Boynton, James SJ	Detroit
Brown, Timothy SJ	Maryland
Buckland, Stephen SJ	Zimbabwe
Busto Sáiz, José Ramón SJ	Castile
Bwanali, Peter SJ	Zambia–Malawi
Calderón, Gustavo SJ	Ecuador
Canillas Lailla, Carlos SJ	Paraguay
Cardó, Carlos SJ	Peru
Cardozo Cortez, René SJ	Bolivia
Carneiro, Carlos SJ	Portugal
Casalone, Carlo SJ	Italy
Case, Frank E. SJ	General Curia
Català Carpintero, Vicent SJ	Aragon
Cavassa Canessa, Ernesto SJ	Peru
Chae, Matthias Joon-ho SJ	Korea
Changanacherry, Jose SJ	Gujarat
Chilinda, Charles SJ	Zambia-Malawi
Chojnacki, Gerald SJ	New York
Cooke, Vincent SJ	New York
Corkery, James SJ	Ireland
Cutinha, Jerome SJ	Jamshedpur
da Silva, Anthony SJ	Goa
Daccache, Salim SJ	Near East
Dacok, Ján SJ	Slovakia
Daoust, Joseph SJ	Detroit
Dardis, John SJ	Ireland
Dartmann, Stefan SJ	Germany

De Luca, Renzo SJ	Japan
de Mello, Francis SJ	Bombay
De Mori, Geraldo SJ	North-East Brazil
Devadoss, Mudiappasamy SJ	Madurai
D'Souza, Charles SJ	Kohima
D'Souza, Jerome SJ	Karnataka
D'Souza, Hector SJ	Karnataka
D'Souza, Lisbert SJ	General Curia
D'Souza, Anthony SJ	Bombay
Dumortier, François-Xavier SJ	France
Dyrek, Krzysztof SJ	South Poland
Echarte Oñate, Ignacio SJ	General Curia
Feely, Thomas SJ	New York
Fernández Franco, Fernando SJ	Gujarat
Fitzgibbons, John SJ	Wisconsin
Follmann, José Ivo SJ	South Brazil
García Jiménez, José Ignacio SJ	Castile
Geisinger, Robert SJ	Chicago
Gellard, Jacques SJ	General Curia
Gendron, Louis SJ	China
Gómez Boulin, Alfonso SJ	Argentina
González Buelta, Benjamín SJ	Cuba
González Modroño, Isidro SJ	Castile
Goussikindey, Eugène SJ	West Africa
Grieu, Etienne SJ	France
Grummer, James E. SJ	Wisconsin
Gudaitis, Aldonas SJ	Lithuania–Lett
Hajduk, Tadeusz SJ	South Poland
Holman, Michael SJ	Britain
Huang, Daniel Patrick L. SJ	Philippines

Hylmar, František SJ	Bohemia
Idiáquez Guevara, José SJ	Central America
Ilboudo, Jean SJ	West Africa
Jaramillo, Roberto SJ	Amazonia
Jeyaraj, Veluswamy SJ	Calcutta
Joseph Sebastian, Sandanam SJ	Andhra
Julien, Jaovory SJ	Madagascar
Kalapura, James SJ	Jamshedpur
Kalubi, Augustin SJ	Central Africa
Kammer, Alfred SJ	New Orleans
Karayampuram, Joy SJ	Patna
Karekezi, Augustin SJ	Rwanda–Burundi
Karla, Viliam SJ	Slovakia
Karumathil, Joye James SJ	Kerala
Kejžar, Franc SJ	Slovenia
Kennedy, Michael SJ	California
Kerhuel, Antoine SJ	France
King, Geoffrey SJ	Australia
Kiyaka, Isaac SJ	Eastern Africa
Koenot, Jan SJ	North Belgium
Kolling, João Geraldo SJ	South Brazil
KOLVENBACH, Peter-Hans SJ	General Curia
Koprek, Ivan SJ	Croatia
Köster, Wendelin SJ	General Curia
Kot, Tomasz SJ	North Poland
Kowalczyk, Dariusz SJ	North Poland
Krettek, Gerald SJ	Wisconsin
Kujur, Joseph SJ	Ranchi
Kuriacose, Thomas SJ	Delhi
Lamboley, Thierry SJ	France

Laporte, Jean-Marc SJ	English Canada
LeBlond, Daniel SJ	French Canada
Lee, Patrick SJ	Oregon
Lee, John SJ	China
Leitner, Severin SJ	Austria
Lewis, Mark SJ	New Orleans
Liberti, Vittorio SJ	Italy
Locatelli, Paul SJ	California
Lombardi, Federico SJ	Italy
Longchamp, Albert SJ	Switzerland
Louis, Prakash SJ	Patna
Lukács, János SJ	Hungary
Mace, John SJ	Wisconsin
Madrzyk, Leszek Andrzej SJ	North Poland
Magadia, Jose SJ	Philippines
Magriñà, Lluis SJ	Tarragon
Maniyar, Lawrence SJ	Nepal
Marcouiller, Douglas SJ	Missouri
Masawe, Fratern SJ	Eastern Africa
McGarry, John SJ	California
McIntosh, Robert SJ	Korea
McMahon, Timothy SJ	Missouri
Menéndez Martínez, Valentín SJ	General Curia
Mercier, Ronald SJ	New England
Messmer, Otto SJ	Russia
Morales Orozco, José SJ	Mexico
Morfín Otero, Carlos SJ	Mexico
Morujão, Manuel SJ	Portugal
Mosca, Juan SJ	Uruguay
Mudavassery, Edward SJ	Hazaribagh

Mukonori, Fidelis SJ	Zimbabwe
Ndombi, Jean-Roger SJ	West Africa
Nebres, Bienvenido SJ	Philippines
Nguyên, Công Đoan Joseph SJ	Vietnam
NICOLÁS, Adolfo SJ	Japan
Ntima, Nkanza SJ	Central Africa
Orbegozo, Jesús SJ	Venezuela
Orozco Hernández, Juan Luis SJ	Mexico
Pace, Paul SJ	Malta
Palacio, Alfonso Carlos SJ	Central Brazil
Pallipalakatt, Varghese SJ	Dumka–Raiganj
Panna, Boniface SJ	Madhya Pradesh
Pappu, Peter SJ	Darjeeling
Parakad, Joseph SJ	Darjeeling
Pattarumadathil, Henry SJ	Kerala
Pattery, George SJ	Calcutta
Polanco Sánchez, Félix SJ	Antillas
Prabhu, Vijay SJ	Karnataka
Priyono Marwan, Agustinus SJ	Indonesia
Puthussery, Varghese SJ	Dumka-Raiganj
Quickley, George SJ	North-West Africa
Rafanambinana, Jean Romain SJ	Madagascar
Raj, Sebasti SJ	Madurai
Raper, Mark SJ	Australia
Recolons de Arquer, Marcos SJ	Bolivia
Regan, Thomas SJ	New England
Restrepo Lince, Alvaro SJ	Colombia
Rhode, Ulrich SJ	Germany
Riyo Mursanto, Robertus Bellarminus SJ	Indonesia
Roach, Thomas SJ	Maryland